Activities and Exercises for Teaching English Pronunciation

This book is a practical, comprehensive tool for busy teachers or educators teaching English pronunciation. Brown puts pronunciation into perspective with other aspects of language, highlighting the importance of teaching pronunciation from the start. Applicable for both British and American pronunciation, this book is organized by aspects of pronunciation and includes a wealth of photocopiable worksheets to use in the classroom. The engaging exercises include rhymes, games, puzzles, narratives, and more, all designed to promote learner engagement and understanding. Each worksheet is accompanied by supplementary resources and guidance, including recommendations for modifying lessons for different English learner proficiency levels; instructions for the teacher and learners; correct or expected answers; and tips for teachers to extend and create their own exercises. The versatility and adaptability of this book make it a beneficial resource for teachers of ESL/EFL/EAL, as well as educational professionals who consult and oversee teacher trainer programs and courses in TESOL.

Adam Brown is Director of Research at the Auckland Institute of Studies, New Zealand.

Activities and Exercises for Teaching English Pronunciation

Adam Brown

Routledge
Taylor & Francis Group
NEW YORK AND LONDON

First published 2022
by Routledge
605 Third Avenue, New York, NY 10158

and by Routledge
2 Park Square, Milton Park, Abingdon, Oxon, OX14 4RN

Routledge is an imprint of the Taylor & Francis Group, an informa business

© 2022 Adam Brown

The right of Adam Brown to be identified as author of this work has been asserted by him in accordance with sections 77 and 78 of the Copyright, Designs and Patents Act 1988.

All rights reserved. The purchase of this copyright material confers the right on the purchasing institution to photocopy or download pages which bear the copyright line at the bottom of the page. No other parts of this book may be reprinted or reproduced or utilized in any form or by any electronic, mechanical, or other means, now known or hereafter invented, including photocopying and recording, or in any information storage or retrieval system, without permission in writing from the publishers.

Trademark notice: Product or corporate names may be trademarks or registered trademarks, and are used only for identification and explanation without intent to infringe.

Library of Congress Cataloging-in-Publication Data
Names: Brown, Adam, 1952– author.
Title: Activities and exercises for teaching English pronunciation / Adam Brown.
Description: New York, NY : Routledge, 2021. | Series: ESL & applied linguistics professional series | Includes bibliographical references.
Identifiers: LCCN 2021009098 (print) | ISBN 9780367551650 (hardback) | ISBN 9780367551629 (paperback) | ISBN 9781003092247 (ebook)
Subjects: LCSH: English language—Pronunciation—Study and teaching. | English language—Study and teaching—Foreign speakers. | English language—Pronunciation of foreign speakers.
Classification: LCC PE1137 .B76 2021 (print) | LCC PE1137 (ebook) | DDC 421/.52071—dc23
LC record available at https://lccn.loc.gov/2021009098
LC ebook record available at https://lccn.loc.gov/2021009099

ISBN: 978-0-367-55165-0 (hbk)
ISBN: 978-0-367-55162-9 (pbk)
ISBN: 978-1-003-09224-7 (ebk)

Typeset in Palatino
by Apex CoVantage, LLC

Access the support material: www.routledge.com/9780367551629

Contents

	Title	Pronunciation focus	Type of exercise	Individual, pair or group
Section A The components of pronunciation				
A1	Who needs good pronunciation?	Pronunciation targets	A form, and discussion	P, G
A2	How do you feel about pronunciation?	Attitudes towards pronunciation, and English	A Monopoly™-style game	G
A3	Who are we?	Suprasegmentals and emotions	Pronunciation, with class feedback	P
A4	Are you Mr. Grumpy?	Suprasegmentals and emotions	Pronunciation, with class feedback	I
A5	Rhubarb	Suprasegmentals and emotions	Dialogs	P
A6	Big and small mistakes	The importance of pronunciation features	A form, and discussion	I
A7	My language or yours?	The distinctiveness of English pronunciation, and learners' native language pronunciation	A listening exercise, identifying the language	I
A8	English with my native voice quality, my native language with English voice quality	The distinctiveness of English pronunciation, and learners' native language pronunciation	Production	I

Section B Suprasegmentals

B1	Waking up for class	Suprasegmentals, especially rhythm, linking	A rap	G
B2	There was a young lady from …	Rhyme	Piecing together limericks	P
B3	And to end the news, …	Key (pause, intonation), "verbal paragraphs"	Analysis, then production	I, P
B4	My name's Sophie	Sentence stress	Production, with learner choice	P
B5	What year? Every year.	Stress and contrast	Production of jokes	I, P, G
B6	What's the difference between a cat and a comma?	Stress and contrast, rhyme	Production of plays-on-words	I, P, G
B7	No, it isn't.	Stress and correction	Production, with learner choice	P
B8	Let's eat Grandpa	Pauses	Analysis, then production of texts.	I, P

Section C Word stress

C1	BRAzil, braZIL?	Stress placement in multisyllable country names	A maze, with analysis of stress placement, then production	I
C2	EDucation, eDUcation, eduCAtion, educaTION?	Stress placement in multisyllable words	A maze, with analysis of stress placement, then production	I
C3	She was presented with a present	Stress placement in noun/verb pairs	A grammar game, followed by production	I
C4	Edinburgh, eDINburgh, edinBURGH?	Stress placement in multisyllable British place names	A maze involving stress-recognition	I

| C5 | Letter from London | Stress placement in multisyllable American state names | A stress-recognition sorting game | I |

Section D Spelling and phonemic symbols

D1	Eh, bee, sea, …	Pronunciation of the names of letters	A sorting game	I
D2	We joined the navy to see the world	Homophones	A mistake-spotting exercise	I, P
D3	Around the world in 20 countries	Recognizing phonemic symbols	A wordsearch of countries of the world (BrE pronunciation)	I
D4	D'you know the capital of Alaska?	Recognizing phonemic symbols	A wordsearch of US state capitals (AmE pronunciation)	I
D5	Let us prey	Homophones	A matching game of homophone jokes	G
D6	Never a cross word	Producing phonemic transcription	A crossword using phonemic symbols	I, P, G

Section E Vowels and consonants

E1	Sounds in common	Identifying sounds in common	A pen-and-paper exercise involving pronouncing	I, P
E2	What's the difference?	Identifying differentiating sounds in minimal pairs	A pen-and-paper exercise involving pronouncing	I, P
E3	Allan or Ellen?	Identifying words containing /æ/	A sound-recognition maze game, with spelling implications	I

E4	Do we invite Yvonne?	Identifying words containing /ɪ/	A sound-recognition game, with spelling implications	I
E5	United or untied?	Identifying words containing /j/	A sound-recognition maze game, with spelling implications	I
E6	Happy hour	Identifying words containing /h/	A sound-recognition maze game, with spelling implications	I
E7	So, do go!	Identifying the odd-one-out in vowels	A pen-and-paper sound-recognition exercise, with spelling implications	I
E8	Who? When? Where?	Identifying the odd-one-out in consonants	A pen-and-paper sound-recognition exercise, with spelling implications	I
E9	A big pig	Plosives /p, b, t, d, k, g/	A communicative sound-distinguishing exercise	P
E10	I sought; I thought; I taught	*th* sounds /θ, ð/	A communicative sound-distinguishing exercise	P
E11	Take the dose, then doze	/s, z/	A communicative sound-distinguishing exercise	P
E12	Jerry ate a jelly	/r, l/	A communicative sound-distinguishing exercise	P

E13	Caesar's scissors	Long and short vowels	A communicative sound-distinguishing exercise	P
E14	We are phonetics fanatics	/e, æ/	A communicative sound-distinguishing exercise	P
E15	Pause, then pose for the camera	Diphthongs	A communicative sound-distinguishing exercise	P

Support Material

Exercises marked with the Support Material symbol have associated audio files which can be downloaded by visiting the book product page on our website: www.routledge.com/9780367551629. Then click on the tab that says "Support Material" and select the files. They will begin downloading to your computer.

The following exercises have corresponding audio files:

A3	Who are we?
A7	My lang or yours
B1	Rap
B2	There was a young lady from . . .
B3	And to end the news, . . .
C1	BRAzil, braZIL?
C3	She was presented with a present
C4	LINcoln, linCOLN?
C5	Alaska, aLASka, alasKA?
D1	Eh, bee, sea, . . .
E1	Sounds in common
E2	What's the difference?
E4	Do we invite Yvonne?

Phonemic Symbols Used

This transcription corresponds to the symbols used by Wells's *Longman Pronunciation Dictionary* (2008).

Two major reference accents are used in this book:

AmE stands for American English, sometimes called General American. It is "what is spoken by the majority of Americans, namely those who do not have a noticeable eastern or southern accent" (Wells, 2008, p. xiv).

BrE stands for British English. It represents standard southern British English—so not Scottish, Welsh, Irish, or other distinctly regional British accents. It is the descendant of Received Pronunciation, and is sometimes called BBC English.

Consonants

p	pen	tʃ	church	s	soon	n	nice
b	back	dʒ	judge	z	zero	ŋ	ring
t	tea	f	fat	ʃ	ship	l	light
d	day	v	view	ʒ	pleasure	r	right
k	key	θ	thing	h	hot	j	yet
g	get	ð	this	m	more	w	wet

Vowels

ɪ	kit	ʌ	strut	u:	goose	ʊə	cure (BrE)*
e	dress	ʊ	foot	aʊ	mouth	ɔ:	thought
æ	trap	i:	fleece	əʊ	goat (BrE)	ɜ:	nurse†
ɒ	lot (BrE)	eɪ	face	oʊ	goat (AmE)	ə	about†
ɑ:	lot (AmE)	ɔɪ	choice	ɪə	near (BrE)*	i	easy, react‡
ɑ:	father			eə	square (BrE)*	u	situation, arduous‡

* In AmE, these words contain a vowel followed by /r/: /nɪr, skwer, kjʊr/.

† AmE pronunciation of *murder* is transcribed /mɜrdər/ in this book, although the two vowel plus /r/ sequences may be realized only by r-coloured vowels.

‡ An unstressed vowel of the /i:, ɪ/ or /u:, ʊ/ quality.

In this book:

- a tilde ("~") is used to show alternative pronunciations between AmE and BrE, e.g. *grass* /græs ~ grɑːs/.

- brackets are used around /r/, to indicate that it is pronounced in AmE but not in BrE (rhotic /r/), e.g. *worth* /wɜː(r)θ/ represents /wɜːrθ/ (AmE) and /wɜːθ/ (BrE).

Introduction

This book contains exercises for the teaching of English pronunciation. It is therefore very practical, with worksheets etc. that are photocopiable and usable in the classroom. They may be immediately usable, or usable after adaptation according to the age, proficiency level, vocabulary level, etc. of the learners. In some cases, versions of the same exercises aimed at different levels of learners are provided here.

This introduction briefly covers a number of background issues that teachers should consider when teaching English pronunciation.

How Languages Are Learned

When we learn our native language(s), we do so largely by imitation of those around us, especially our parents, older siblings, etc. These people are proficient in the language, but may have little understanding of exactly what they are modeling—where the tongue is, what the vocal cords are doing, etc. Similarly, we learn our native language(s) at a very early age, before we have the intellectual capacity to understand exactly what is being taught. It is mostly by imitation.

When we learn another language, the situation is different in three main ways. Firstly, by definition, we have already learned a language—our native language. The sounds of our native language have been mastered, and have become second nature to us. A willingness to adapt to the sounds of the new language—some of them totally new, some of them different in subtle ways—is therefore necessary.

Secondly, other languages are learned at a later age than our native language. Children typically master all the major features of their native language by the time they go to primary school. Other languages are typically taught in secondary school. Many people learn other languages at even later ages, perhaps because the languages are useful for business, or because the people want to get by when they go abroad on holiday.

Thirdly, we learn our native languages by listening to others around us, especially our parents. However, other languages are normally learned by explicit instruction from a teacher. In an educational environment, and especially in higher levels of education, with learners of older ages, imitation still works, but it is often accompanied by more explicit explanation of what is happening when we produce sounds.

Explanation naturally means that the teacher must understand in some detail what is happening. Simply being able to speak the language is not enough. That is, there is a difference between knowing a language, and knowing about a language.

Teaching Pronunciation Versus Other Aspects of Language

There are two problems about teaching pronunciation that do not apply, or do not apply so much, in other aspects of language teaching.

Firstly, there are many strands that make up pronunciation. These are summarized in Figure 1.1, and discussed further later in this section.

Secondly, all the strands occur at the same time in speech, and therefore need to be taught as soon as possible. You cannot, for example, postpone teaching the /ð/ sound, a voiced dental fricative, because it is difficult for most learners; it is a very common sound in English, occurring in a lot of common words: *the, this, that, they, there*, etc. You can, however, postpone teaching advanced aspects of grammar, for instance the past perfect tense (*I had done something*), until long after learners have mastered easier, more common tenses (the simple present, simple past, present continuous, etc.). In short, several features of pronunciation need to be taught from the very start.

The Components of Pronunciation

The various components that go together to make up pronunciation are shown in Figure 1.1.

Let us start at the right-hand side of the diagram, with the most-evident features of pronunciation: the vowel and consonant sounds. These are known as the segmentals, or segments, because they are the basic building blocks.

Vowel sounds are traditionally divided into monophthongs (where the position of the tongue and lips does not change, e.g. /ɑː/) and diphthongs (where there is movement, e.g. /aɪ/). However, they can also be divided into short vowels (which are monophthongs because they are short, e.g. /ɪ/) and long vowels. Long vowels may be long monophthongs, e.g. /ɑː/, or long diphthongs, e.g. /aɪ/. This division is preferable because long monophthongs and long diphthongs often function in similar ways.

Figure 1.1 The components of pronunciation

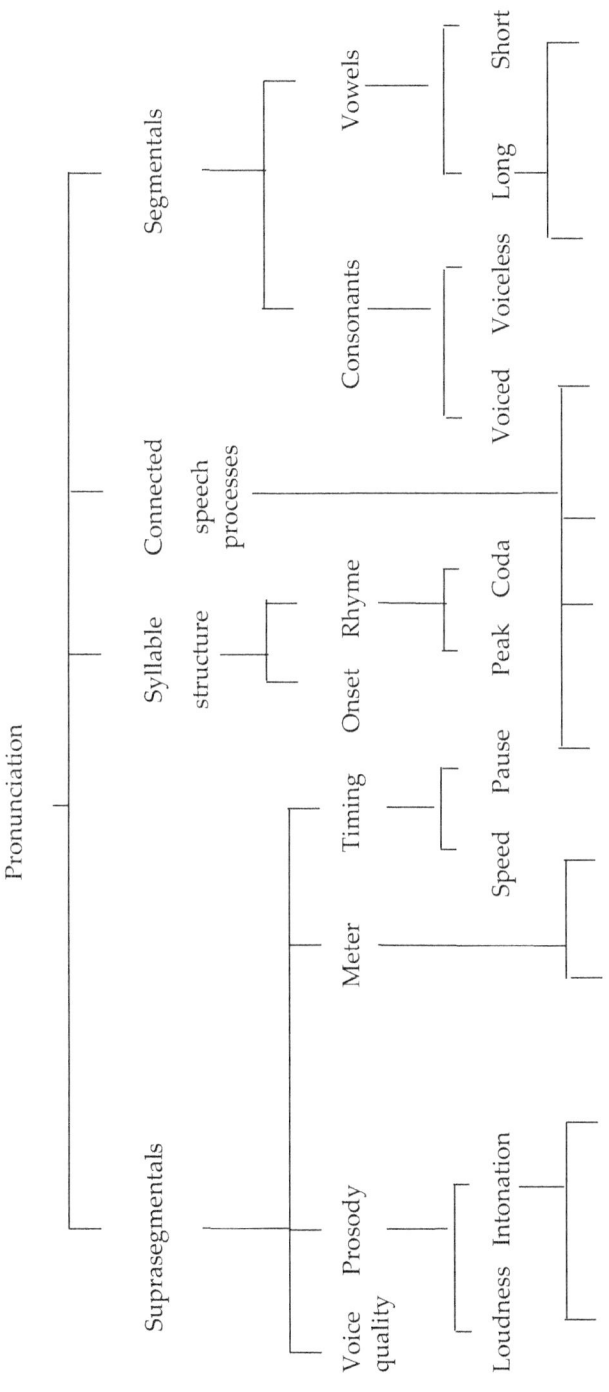

- Pronunciation
  - Suprasegmentals
    - Voice quality
    - Prosody
      - Loudness
      - Intonation
        - Pitch range
        - Pitch movement
    - Meter
      - Word stress
      - Rhythm
    - Timing
      - Speed
      - Pause
  - Syllable structure
    - Onset
    - Rhyme
      - Peak
      - Coda
  - Connected speech processes
    - Assimilation
    - Elision
    - Linking
    - Weak forms
  - Segmentals
    - Consonants
      - Voiced
      - Voiceless
    - Vowels
      - Long
        - Diphthongs
        - Long monophthongs
      - Short

Introduction ◆ 3

Consonant sounds are traditionally divided into those that are voiced (involving vibration of the vocal cords), and voiceless (without this vibration). This division makes sense in that voiced consonants behave like other voiced consonants, and voiceless like voiceless. However, the voicing feature—whether the vocal cords are vibrating or not—is often not the most reliable feature to concentrate on.

At the other extreme, on the left-hand side of the diagram, suprasegmentals are those features that are imposed on (supra) the string of vowel and consonant sound segments.

Not all writers would agree with the division of suprasegmentals into voice quality, prosody, meter, and timing. However, they would agree with the features that come under those headings.

Voice quality refers to long-term settings of the various vocal organs. Voice quality features thus affect all susceptible segments in the speech. They include settings of the vocal cords, e.g. creaky voice, whisperiness. They may also relate to settings of the soft palate, allowing air into or stopping it from the nasal cavity, e.g. the nasal speech of Birmingham, UK. Settings of the tongue affect all vowel sounds, e.g. the velarization of Liverpool speech, whereby all vowels are slightly retracted from their positions in other accents. Labialization refers to the amount of rounding or spreading of the lips as an overall setting.

Different writers include different features under the umbrella term *prosody*. Loudness is a simple concept easily understood. Intonation, however, is more complex and relates to the pitch or note at which speech is produced, which varies throughout the stretch of speech. The pitch depends on the rate of vibration of the vocal cords and, as a result, only voiced sounds can be said to have pitch. We can distinguish pitch range (the typical highest and lowest pitch of a speaker) from pitch movement (how pitch goes up and down within that range).

Meter refers to the rhythm of speech. At least in one often-quoted analysis of rhythm, it depends on the regularity of stressed syllables. Word stress, or the placement of stress on particular syllables within words, is therefore an important factor in rhythm.

Timing relates to the temporal characteristics of speech. Speed distinguishes between fast and slow speech. Pause represents the absence of speech, which thus affects the perception of how fast the speech is.

Between the two extremes of segmentals and suprasegmentals lie other features related to the way that segmentals combine in connected speech.

Speakers, regardless of their native language, seem to have the concept of a syllable, although it is not an easy one to define rigorously. Words may have only one syllable (e.g. *one* /wʌn/), or more than one (e.g. *twenty* /twenti/). Within each syllable, any initial consonant(s) is known as the onset (/w, tw, t/ in the words *one*, *twenty* above). The remainder is the rhyme (/ʌn, en, i/), which is the part that determines rhymes in poetry; for instance, *one* rhymes with *son, pun,* and *done*, regardless of the differences in spelling. The rhyme can itself be divided into the peak (the vowel) and the coda (any final consonant(s)); thus, /ʌ, e, i/ above are the peaks, while /n/ is a coda in two of the syllables.

As their name implies, connected speech processes describe the way sounds may be affected by adjacent sounds, when the speech is connected and pronounced at a normal, relatively fast speed.

Assimilation means that one sound changes in some respect in order to become similar to the adjacent, usually following, sound, e.g. *Great Britain* /greɪt brɪtən/ > /greɪp brɪtən/.

Elision is the deletion of sounds in certain contexts, e.g. *best friend* /best frend/ > /bes frend/.

Words and syllables are not separate from the words and syllables that surround them. There is no small pause between words, corresponding to the space in writing. Instead, the ends of words and syllables are linked up to the beginning of the following words and syllables. For instance, there is a joke in pronunciation circles about a young man who went into a shop. "I'd like to buy a potato clock, please." "I don't think we sell any such thing." "Oh, what a pity, because I am starting a new job on Monday and my boss told me to get a potato clock." Of course, the boss told him to "get up at eight o'clock." Linking (as well as other features like weakening) makes the two meanings pronounced much the same.

The alternation between words that are stressed in sentences and those that are not depends on the stressed words being pronounced clearly and, just as importantly, the unstressed words not being pronounced clearly. This often happens with grammatical function words like *an, and, from, have, of, them*. Most of the time they are unstressed (because no emphasis is being given to them) and pronounced with the /ə/ vowel, rather than a full, strong vowel. This is occasionally reflected in the spelling, e.g. *fish 'n' chips*.

This has necessarily been a brief description of a wide field. For greater detail, see Brown (2014).

What Do Learners Learn in Pronunciation Classes?

Bloom's taxonomy is a categorization of educational learning objectives, named after US educational psychologist Benjamin Bloom, who devised it in the 1950s. Despite being well over half a century old, it is still found useful and influential by those in the teaching profession. Slight modifications to it have been suggested over the years. It essentially describes what learners acquire on a course of study, that they did not have, or could not do so well, at the start. These objectives are divided into three broad domains.

The *cognitive* domain relates to knowledge, i.e. information, facts, and figures. This information is learned simply by understanding and remembering it. A few of the exercises in this book concern this domain, for example, the various possible spellings for the /ɪ/ vowel sound (exercise E4).

Pronunciation is a physical skill involving the coordinated movement of the various parts of the lungs, vocal cords, mouth, and nose. The *skills* domain comprises this. Just as the best way to improve at football is to practice playing football and learn from your mistakes and shortcomings, so the best way to improve your pronunciation is to actually pronounce. For this reason, exercises in this book involve production; that is, saying things out loud, either explicitly in the exercise itself (e.g. the communicative minimal pairs in E9–15), or in the debrief (e.g. the /æ/ and confusable vowel sounds in E3).

Finally, the *affective* domain relates to feelings, attitudes, emotions, etc. For instance, the first two exercises (A1, A2) promote discussion of how learners feel about English, and English pronunciation.

In short, the cognitive domain relates to what you know, the skills domain to what you can do, and the affective domain to how you feel. All three are important. However, as primarily a physical activity, the skills domain should not be overlooked. Learners cannot learn pronunciation if they are not instructed to pronounce things out loud.

The Non-Native Speaker as English Teacher

Readers who are not native speakers of English may feel that they are at a disadvantage when it comes to teaching English, including pronunciation. This is not necessarily the case.

Native speakers have native-speaker pronunciation. Some non-native speaker-teachers of English may have excellent pronunciation, but most have a pronunciation that diverges from native pronunciation to varying degrees.

Native speakers have large vocabularies of words they actively use. They also know how to pronounce these words correctly, in terms of the vowels and consonants, stress placement, etc. Non-native speaker-teachers are likely to have smaller vocabularies. They may also mispronounce some words, being deceived by the inconsistencies of English spelling.

In contrast, on the plus side, non-native speaker-teachers have some advantages over native speakers. Non-native speakers have learned English in addition to their native language. They therefore understand the similarities and differences between the two languages, and the difficulties that learners face, because they have faced them themselves. A native speaker of, say, Chinese thus has a natural advantage teaching English to Chinese learners, over a native English speaker.

Similarly, a non-native speaker-teacher has learned English through explicit instruction, whereas a native speaker has not. A native speaker may speak the language perfectly (natively), but that does not mean that they know a lot about the language. As a result, they may not be able to explain points about the language, including pronunciation. A non-native speaker may be able to explain the features and rules of English better, because these features and rules were explained to them when they learned English.

American and British Pronunciation

The exercises in the suprasegmental Sections A, B, and C work, whether the reference used in the classroom is AmE (American English) or BrE (British English). While there are geographical differences in the vowel and consonant segmentals in Sections D and E, the exercises have been written so that they work in either AmE or BrE, with very few exceptions (e.g. D3 and D4).

Guidelines to Exercises

At the beginning of each exercise, several factors relating to the exercise are discussed.

The *Pronunciation point* explains what aspect of pronunciation the exercise focuses on. These explanations are deliberately kept brief and simple. This is to help the teacher to conduct the exercise appropriately. There is no intention that any of this should necessarily be conveyed to the learners.

The *Minimum level* shows what proficiency the learners need in order to tackle the exercise. Only two levels are used: elementary and intermediate. No more sophisticated categorization is needed, e.g. lower intermediate, upper intermediate. In any case, the level depends on the learners—their age and maturity, etc.

The *Exercise type* briefly describes what kind of activity it is.

For each exercise, *Approximate time* gives an indication of how long the exercise might last in class. These timings are necessarily variable, since they depend on the number of learners in the class, the proficiency level of the learners, the vocabulary level of the learners, whether the learners are adults or younger, etc. Nevertheless, the relative length of time—whether the exercise is likely to take a whole one-hour class, or whether it is a ten-minute quickie—is accurate. In any case, pronunciation work can be exhausting for the learners, and should not fill up whole classes. Very few of the exercises in this book are longer than 30 minutes.

Preparation alerts the teacher to materials that need to be prepared beforehand: what materials, how many, etc. Nowadays many learners bring devices (laptops, tablets, etc.) to class. Instead of printed materials, the exercise can be presented in soft copy on their devices. For some exercises, the materials can be shown to the whole class by projector.

In *Introducing the exercise*, some suggestions are made as to how the teacher can initiate the exercise. Often, this takes the form of explaining things such as the format of raps and limericks, or pronunciation features such as word stress. It may involve explaining some vocabulary, or differences between AmE and BrE.

Conducting the exercise is a step-by-step guide for the teacher. This covers whether the activity is conducted individually, in pairs, or in groups. In pairs or groups, the teacher must understand how materials are distributed. Most importantly, it explains what the learners do. This is not, however, a "painting by numbers" approach; the teacher can adapt the procedure according to the learners, their needs, their proficiency, what has preceded the exercise, etc.

Debrief notes describe what happens, if anything, after the learners have attempted the exercise. In many exercises, this is the most important part, because it recaps the main pronunciation points. In one or two cases, a second exercise, subsequent to the main one, is included in order to make further points. Often, it is suggested that all the words in the exercise should be pronounced by the class. The spelling-to-sound and sound-to-spelling correspondences of English vowels and consonants may also be deduced from the examples given.

It is impossible to write pronunciation materials that are appropriate for all learners at all levels in all situations. The *Create your own materials* suggestion encourages teachers to produce their own materials that are better tailored to the precise group of learners being taught. These original materials may be modifications of the exercises given here, or may be different exercises inspired by the type of exercise here.

The title of exercise E10 (*I sought; I thought; I taught*) is, in fact, a reasonable definition of this kind of research. Firstly, you identify a problem and look for background information about it, or even elicit your own data by research. Then you consider what you have found and analyze it, coming up with possible solutions to the problem. Research for research's sake is meaningless, unless it somehow benefits your learners. That is, you make their learning more effective, more efficient, longer-lasting, faster, etc.

That is what the *Create your own materials* subsection in each exercise attempts to promote. Firstly (*seek*), work out what pronunciation features your learners have difficulty with. Find out how important these features are for communication. For instance, for the sounds in E10 (/t, θ/), how common are these sounds in connected speech and how many words are distinguished by them (minimal pairs)? A good place to start is Higgins (2017). Read up on the phonologies of your learners' native languages.

Secondly (*think*), analyze what you have found. Many pronunciation problems are caused by differences between English and the learners' native language. Not many languages have the /θ/ consonant, so it is a new sound for many learners. Devise exercises that use the sounds in question.

Finally (*teach*), try out your original materials on your learners. They may work well. On the other hand, they may not, in which case some tinkering is probably necessary.

Integration of Pronunciation Work

Consider integrating pronunciation work into other English language work. When learners learn new vocabulary, they must also learn the pronunciation of the words. Certain grammar points have implications for pronunciation, e.g. the different pronunciations of the past tense ending in *wished, hugged, wanted*. Many of the exercises in this book involve passages. Different passages can be substituted, including passages that are being used for other language work. This is also an opportunity to use some English literature in pronunciation work, taking into account the level of the text and the level of the learners.

Technology

The exercises in this book are intended to be carried out in face-to-face situations. Typically, this will be in the classroom with a teacher. Nowadays, some teaching is carried out online. The exercises can be used online, although some adaptation to the online environment may be necessary. The exercises are, nevertheless, still face-to-face.

Technological advances have allowed online sources and smartphone apps to be developed for pronunciation, for use by the learner without teacher involvement. This is beyond the scope of this book of face-to-face exercises. Interested readers can consult the Pennington and Rogerson-Revell, and Yoshida references in the bibliography, as well as many other sources to be found online.

Further Reading

This has been a necessarily brief introduction to the features of English pronunciation, and factors related to pronunciation teaching. The literature below goes into greater detail for those readers wanting to delve deeper.

Bloom, B. S., Engelhart, M. D., Furst, E. J., Hill, W. H. & Krathwohl, D. R. (1956). *Taxonomy of educational objectives: The classification of educational goals. Handbook I: Cognitive domain*. David McKay Company.

Brown, A. (2014). *Pronunciation and phonetics: A practical guide for English language teachers*. Routledge.
Brown, A. (2019). *Understanding and teaching English spelling: A strategic guide*. Routledge.
Celce-Murcia, M., Brinton, D. M. & Goodwin, J. M. (2010). *Teaching pronunciation: A course book and reference guide* (2nd edition). Cambridge University Press.
Davies, A. (2013). *Native speakers and native users: Loss and gain*. Cambridge University Press.
Grant, L. (Ed.). (2014). *Pronunciation myths*. University of Michigan Press.
Hall, C. & Hastings, C. (2017). *Phonetics, phonology and pronunciation for the language classroom*. Red Globe Press/Macmillan.
Hancock, M. (2020). *Mark Hancock's 50 tips for teaching pronunciation*. Cambridge University Press.
Higgins, J. (2017). *Minimal pairs for English RP*. http://minimal.marlodge.net/minimal.html
Higgins, J. (2018). *English (RP) homophones*. http://minimal.marlodge.net/phone.html
Isaacs, T. & Trofimovich, P. (Eds.). (2017). *Second language pronunciation assessment: Interdisciplinary perspectives*. Multilingual Matters.
Jones, T. (Ed.). (2016). *Pronunciation in the classroom: The overlooked essential*. TESOL.
Jones, T. (2019). *Fifty ways to teach pronunciation: Tips for ESL/EFL teachers*. Independently published (ISBN: 1691712418).
Kang, O., Thomson, R. I. & Murphy, J. M. (Eds.). (2017). *The Routledge handbook of contemporary English pronunciation*. Routledge.
Krathwohl, D. R. (2002). A revision of Bloom's taxonomy: An overview. Theory into Practice, 41(4), 212–218. https://doi.org/10.1207/s15430421tip4104_2
Levis, J. M. (2018). *Intelligibility, oral communication, and the teaching of pronunciation*. Cambridge University Press.
Marks, J. & Bowen, T. (2012). *The book of pronunciation: Proposals for a practical pedagogy*. Delta Publishing.
Murphy, J. (2013). *Teaching pronunciation*. TESOL.
Murphy, J. M. (Ed.). (2017). *Teaching the pronunciation of English: Focus on whole courses*. University of Michigan Press.
Newton, J. M. & Nation, I. S. P. (2021). *Teaching ESL/EFL listening and speaking* (2nd edition). Routledge.
Pennington, M. C. (2021). *The pronunciation book: A language teacher's guide*. Equinox Publishing.
Pennington, M. C. & Rogerson-Revell, P. (2019) Using technology for pronunciation teaching, learning, and assessment. In M. C. Pennington & P. Rogerson-Revell (Eds.), *English pronunciation*

teaching and research. Contemporary perspectives (pp. 235–286). Palgrave Macmillan.

Pickering, L. (2018). *Discourse intonation: A discourse-pragmatic approach to teaching the pronunciation of English.* University of Michigan Press.

Reed, M. & Levis, J. M. (Eds.). (2015). *The handbook of English pronunciation.* Wiley-Blackwell.

Walker, R. (2010). *Teaching the pronunciation of English as a lingua franca.* Oxford University Press.

Wells, J. C. (2008). *Longman pronunciation dictionary* (3rd edition). Longman.

Yoshida, M. T. (2018). Choosing technology tools to meet pronunciation teaching and learning goals. *CATESOL Journal, 30*(1), 195–212. https://files.eric.ed.gov/fulltext/EJ1174226.pdf

Section A
The Components of Pronunciation

A1

Who Needs Good Pronunciation?

Pronunciation point: If you don't know what you're aiming for, how can you know if you've achieved it? Not everyone needs a pronunciation of English (or any other foreign language) that is "perfect" or quasi-native. In many circumstances, a target that is lower than this is perfectly acceptable—and probably more likely to be achieved.

Also, mastering English involves not only pronunciation, but also grammar, vocabulary, etc. Teachers do not have unlimited class time to cover everything, so a clear understanding, by both teachers and learners, helps to prioritize elements of language. Participants should be encouraged to try to work out what makes a "perfect" pronunciation desirable or unnecessary, given the circumstance.

Minimum level: Elementary

Exercise type: A thinking and discussion exercise. Learners should therefore discuss the items in pairs or small groups.

Approximate time: 20 minutes (exercise), 20 minutes (debrief)

Preparation: Make one copy of the worksheet for each learner. Alternatively, to save paper, either make the worksheet accessible in soft copy on learners' devices, or show the worksheet on a screen.

Introducing the exercise: Explain that learners do not necessarily need to aim for a perfect pronunciation, but rather one that is widely understood. In any case, many learners are unlikely to achieve perfection.

Conducting the exercise: Distribute the worksheets (or show it on screen). Instruct the learners to discuss in pairs and tick one column each time. There is no one "right" answer, so encourage students to discuss.

Debrief notes:

The purpose of this exercise is to get learners thinking about their goals in learning English. The level of English pronunciation that people require depends on various factors:

- Whether there is a clear (present or future) audience that the person speaks to. For example, Miss Japan will go the Miss World/Universe pageant, which is conducted in English and where good English pronunciation is a distinct advantage.
- Intelligibility to a wide range of audiences. Immigration officials, hotel frontline staff, flight attendants, taxi drivers, etc. can expect to have to speak to, and be easily intelligible to, tourists from various countries.
- Whether the person is representing his/her country ("flying the flag"). The Malaysian ambassador represents his/her country, and any poor English pronunciation would reflect badly on the country as a whole.
- Proximity to a native English-speaking country. A McDonald's server at Schiphol Airport in Amsterdam is likely to have to deal with many customers from the UK.
- Whether the country is one like (i) the USA and UK, where English is a native language spoken by the vast majority of the population, (ii) India, Malaysia, and Nigeria, in which English, as a former colonial language, has some official functions, such as in education, the media, and the law, or (iii) most of the rest of the world, where English is not a native language but is widespread for international communication, especially for trade. (This three-way model of Englishes around the world comes from Braj Kachru, and is less ambiguous than the perhaps more common terms ENL, ESL, and EFL, English as a native/second/foreign language.)
- Whether school subjects are taught (fully or partly) in English.
- Whether there are serious potential consequences to poor pronunciation. A pilot who is difficult to understand may cause a crash. A spy who does not sound quasi-native will be suspected.

Perhaps the most difficult item to answer in the worksheet is "a school student in your home country." At primary level, students often learn the basics of the language with no clear idea of whom they will eventually speak it with, if ever. In ELT circles, this is sometimes called TENOR "Teaching English for no obvious reason." At secondary level, future requirements may become clearer. For instance, students may decide that they want to go to university in Australia.

Worksheet

Get into pairs. Discuss, and decide whether the following people need a pronunciation of English which is good or very good, or which can be so-so. Tick one column each time.

	So-so	Good	Very good
1. An immigration official at Suvarnabhumi Airport, Bangkok, Thailand			
2. The winner of the Miss Japan beauty contest			
3. A Nigerian teacher of mathematics			
4. A receptionist at the Golden Camel Hotel, Dubai, UAE			
5. A spy from a non-English-speaking country			
6. A teacher of English in PR China			
7. A Pakistani pilot on Pakistan International Airlines			
8. A McDonald's server at Schiphol Airport, Amsterdam, the Netherlands			
9. A Nigerian teacher of English			
10. A Cathay Pacific Airways (Hong Kong) flight attendant			
11. A Singaporean police officer			
12. A newsreader on Bangladesh Television (BTV) English news			
13. The Malaysian ambassador to the UK			
14. A school student in your home country			
15. A taxi driver in Seoul, South Korea			

* This page is photocopiable for classroom use only.

A2

How Do You Feel About Pronunciation?

Pronunciation point: Pronouncing a foreign language can be an emotional experience presenting a psychological barrier to the learner. It is good for learners to discuss among themselves how they feel about English pronunciation. The board game format of this exercise forces learners to express their feelings.

The purpose of this exercise is really to encourage learners to think and talk about English pronunciation in a non-threatening environment.

Minimum level: Intermediate

Exercise type: A game, in the style of Monopoly™, to be played in small groups

Approximate time: 30 minutes (exercise), 20 minutes (debrief)

Preparation: Make enough copies of the board game for the class to carry out the exercise in groups of four or five. So that it can be easily seen, make the copies A3 size. You will also need dice and a counter for each player. The counters can be, for example, small colorful dinosaurs or farm animals from any toy shop.

Introducing the exercise: Explain, especially with a class of disparate learners, that they may all have very different attitudes towards English pronunciation.

Conducting the exercise: Give each group of four or five learners one copy of the board game, four or five counters, and one die. They start at the "start" square, throw the die, move their counter, and answer the question in the box. Encourage them to be honest; there are no right or wrong answers. This discussion need not be overheard by the teacher. It can, if necessary, be in the learners' native language.

The game continues until it is clear that most of the boxes have been discussed.

Debrief notes: Go through all 18 questions, asking the learners to give feedback about the answers that were given, and any discussions. Try to create a non-threatening environment in the classroom, so that learners will happily take part in pronunciation exercises.

Start	1 Which do you prefer: American or British English pronunciation? Why?	2 Has anyone ever mispronounced your name? How did you feel about that?	3 Give three adjectives to describe your pronunciation of English.	4 What is the best way to improve your English pronunciation outside the classroom?	5 Has anyone ever not understood you when you were speaking in English?	6 In the future, who will you speak English to?	↱
18 Do you have "a good ear", or do you prefer pronunciation things to be explained?							7 Name one famous person you think has a horrible accent of English.
17 Name one person you think has a nice accent of English.							8 In what situations is it most important to pronounce well?
16 How do you feel when a foreigner pronounces your language well?							9 What would you say to a foreign speaker who apologizes for their poor accent?
↰	15 Is it more important to have good pronunciation when you are speaking to native English-speaking people or non-native?	14 Are you hoping to speak with a "perfect" English pronunciation?	13 Describe one thing you remember about English pronunciation in your school classes so far.	12 A foreigner doesn't speak your language well and is difficult to understand. What do you do?	11 Are you comfortable speaking English aloud? Why, or why not?	10 If people misunderstand you, how do you repeat yourself in a way that they will understand?	

* This page is photocopiable for classroom use only.

A3

Who Are We?

Pronunciation point: There is much more to pronunciation, and to overall expressiveness, than pronouncing the vowels and consonants accurately, and putting stress in the right place. This exercise focusing on suprasegmentals hopefully convinces learners of this.

Minimum level: Intermediate

Exercise type: A pairwork speaking exercise, where the learners make a choice

Approximate time: 10 minutes (preparation, rehearsal), 30 minutes (exercise), 10 minutes (debrief)

Preparation: Make one copy of the worksheet and one copy of the answer table for each learner.

Introducing the exercise: Explain that, while vowels and consonants are important, they do not lead to expressiveness. You could ask the learners how they express feelings such as surprise, anger, secrecy, etc. in their own language.

Conducting the exercise: Divide the class into pairs. Allocate dialogues to pairs. Tell the learners in each pair to choose one of the alternative sets of characters and contexts below for their dialogue, but not to tell anyone else in the class. For example, the pair with dialogue 1 can choose that "B loves spicy Indian food" or that "B doesn't really like spicy Indian food, but will agree to go with A." The dialogue works, whichever set they choose.

  Give the learners five minutes to rehearse pronouncing their dialogue in an appropriate way for the characters and context they have chosen.

  Ask the first pair to read the dialogue out to the rest of the class in an appropriate way for the characters and context they have chosen. They cannot use gestures or props—only their voices. This is like actors rehearsing a play.

The rest of the learners act as the audience and try to guess which set of characters and context they chose. They mark their guesses with a tick in the answer table. They should also note down in the final column any aspects of the pair's performance that helped them make up their mind. These are important, and should be comments about the pronunciation (not vocabulary, grammar, etc.). They should not be vague ("They sounded secretive"), but focus on particular pronunciation features ("They were whispering").

Repeat this with all the other pairs.

Debrief notes: After all the pairs have acted, ask the learners whether they thought the first pair had chosen the first or second set of characters and contexts. The number of correct answers is an indication of how well the pair acted. Also ask the learners for the pronunciation clues that helped them make up their mind.

Make a checklist on the board of these clues. They will probably cover suprasegmentals such as speed (e.g. slow for more serious matters), loudness (e.g. louder for urgency), intonation (e.g. wider ranges with higher pitches for more animated speech), and voice quality (e.g. whisperiness for secrecy).

Create your own materials: Two-way dialogues like this are not difficult to create. However, you need some ingenuity in thinking of the two scenarios in which the dialogue works. This may involve rather vague expressions in the dialogue, that can be interpreted in different ways in the two situations.

Worksheet 1

Passage 1

A: Shall we go out for a meal?
B: OK. Where?
A: There's a new Indian restaurant in Grange Street.
B: Indian?
A: Yes. I think the food will be similar to the Taj Mahal restaurant in King Street.
B: Their food is really hot and spicy.
A: They have a whole range of different dishes.
B: OK.
A: Let me phone up and make a reservation.
B: Right.

Passage 2

A: Come on. Just give it a try.
B: I can't.
A: I'm sure you can. It's really not that difficult.
B: Do you really think I can do it?
A: Yes, of course you can. It's just a matter of concentration.
B: It's not as easy as you think, you know.
A: Nonsense. Just remember all the coaching you've had.
B: Right. One last try, and then I'm giving up.
A: That's the spirit! If everyone else can do it, surely you can.
B: OK. Here goes. Just let me focus.

Passage 3

A: Where did you go?
B: I went round the hill.
A: And then?
B: All the way to the windmill.
A: Yes, and then?
B: Past Mr. Green's farm.
A: The one next to the dairy?
B: Yes. And then back over the bridge.
A: And how do you feel?
B: I'm thirsty.

* This page is photocopiable for classroom use only.

Passage 4

A: OK. Tell me. What is your name?
B: [Silence]
A: Come on. We need to know.
B: Jill Sanderson.
A: And who did you come here to meet?
B: Michael Jackson.
A: Michael Jackson! Is that his real name?
B: That's the name that I was given. I don't know if it's his real name.
A: Hmmm. And at what time were you supposed to meet him?
B: A quarter past ten, underneath the clock.

Passage 5

A: You'll never guess what happened to me yesterday.
B: What?
A: Well, I was walking out of the bus station, and I was just outside that drinks stall, you know . . .
B: Mmmm.
A: . . . when whom should I meet but Joan Robinson. You remember, that girl who used to work at the supermarket when we lived in the east.
B: Aha.
A: You know what she's been doing in the last three years or so, don't you?
B: What's that?
A: She's on that TV show . . . what's it called . . . that funny show on Friday evenings.
B: I don't know.
A: *Be My Guest*, that's it, that show that's set in a hotel.
B: Really?
A: Yes, but I don't think she remembered me.

* This page is photocopiable for classroom use only.

Passage 6

A: What do you think?
B: I think we'd better tell him.
A: I'm not so sure.
B: Well, if we don't, he'll probably find out some other way.
A: Hmmm. And if he does, he'll be angry that we didn't tell him.
B: Yes. Besides, we might find out that he already suspects it.
A: And in any case, I feel that we *ought* to tell him.
B: Agreed. So, when do we do it?
A: Straight away, I suppose. Could you do it? You're so much better than me at this sort of thing.
B: Oh, OK. Come on, let's go and break the news.

Passage 7

A: We're going to let you go.
B: Thank you very much!
A: I know it's not the news that you thought you were going to hear.
B: You can say that again!
A: The management team discussed it for a long time.
B: Was I the only one you considered?
A: There were one or two possible candidates, but . . . well, we finally agreed on you.
B: That's just great!
A: So you'd better go and start packing.
B: I'll go and tell my wife straight away.

Passage 8

A: Did you get through to him?
B: Yes. I talked to him. It was lucky as he was about to go out.
A: And . . . ?
B: And he said he was coming.
A: You gave him the address, didn't you?
B: Of course I did. In any case, I'm fairly certain that he knows where we live.
A: But people often confuse Cook Street with Cook Avenue on the other side of town.
B: No, I told him it was Cook Street, and that we're just round the corner from the Galaxy cinema. He said he knew where to come.
A: He's got a car, hasn't he?
B: Of course he has. Don't worry, it's all been taken care of.

* This page is photocopiable for classroom use only.

Passage 9

A: How long have you been here?
B: About twenty minutes.
A: Oh dear.
B: Why, what's the problem?
A: Have you seen Lizzy?
B: No, not since this morning.
A: This morning?
B: Why, what's wrong?
A: I'm really worried.
B: Perhaps you should call the police.

Passage 10

A: There are four of us already. We need a fifth. Someone to do the driving.
B: What about George again?
A: What do you mean "again"?
B: He was with us a couple of years ago. He did the driving then.
A: Was he reliable? Did everyone in the team get on with him?
B: Yes. No problems.
A: Then I'll ask Jim to have a word with him . . . try to persuade him.
B: Right.
A: How long do you think we should give him to think it over?
B: Well, the thing's planned for the week after next, so we need an answer fairly soon.

* This page is photocopiable for classroom use only.

Worksheet 2

Decide if the pair have acted the passage in the first or second situation, and tick the "Guess" column. Importantly, write in the "Notes" column about how you made this decision.

	Alternative characters and contexts	Guess	Notes
1	B loves spicy Indian food.		
	B doesn't really like spicy Indian food, but will agree to go with A, rather unwillingly.		
2	The operator of a bungee jump (A) encourages a customer (B).		
	A father (A) tries to persuade his son (B) to do some difficult mathematics homework.		
3	On a picnic, a mother (A) asks her young son/daughter (B) where he/she walked. She's been worried about him/her.		
	A trainer (A) asks an athlete (B) where he ran.		
4	The Secret Service (A) are questioning someone (B) they think is a spy.		
	Airport security (A) are talking to a ten-year-old unaccompanied traveler (B). Nobody is at the airport to meet him/her.		
5	B is reading a newspaper and doesn't want to be disturbed.		
	B went to school with Joan's sister, so is really interested.		
6	Two doctors decide whether to tell a patient he has cancer.		
	Two schoolchildren decide whether to tell the principal that they have broken a window.		
7	The sports team manager (A) has chosen B as a replacement on their Japanese tour, for a player who has been injured.		
	Because of financial problems, the company is having to fire some staff. A breaks the bad news to B.		
8	A husband (B) and wife (A) invite a friend to a dinner party.		
	A husband (B) phones for the doctor for his pregnant wife (A) who has gone into labor.		
9	A snake charmer in a circus (A) asks a colleague (B) about his missing python, Lizzy.		
	A husband (A) had an argument with his wife Lizzy last evening, and asks his housekeeper (B) about her.		
10	Members of a football team are planning a minibus holiday.		
	Members of a gang are planning a robbery.		

* This page is photocopiable for classroom use only.

A4
Are You Mr. Grumpy?

The *Mr. Men* (pronounced "Mister Men") are a series of children's books with male characters, originally produced in the 1970s by British author Roger Hargreaves. A series with female characters, *Little Miss*, appeared in the 1980s (Mr. Men, Little Miss, 2020). After Roger's death in 1988, his son Adam continued to write and illustrate the books. They have been translated into many languages, and sold millions of copies worldwide.

Pronunciation point: As in A3, this exercise focuses on suprasegmentals (intonation, speed, voice quality, etc.).

Some learners seem to lapse into a monotonous delivery when speaking a foreign language (English). However, when the class is over, and they are talking to their friends in their native language, they are very animated and expressive! Emphasize that this expressiveness is appropriate in English too. You could even ask the learners to act out one or two of the scenarios in their native language. You may well find that the pronunciation features used for emotions are similar to, if not the same as, in English.

Minimum level: Intermediate

Exercise type: A individual production exercise, much like acting

Approximate time: 15 minutes (pre-teaching), 20 minutes (exercise), 10 minutes (debrief)

Preparation: Make one copy of Worksheet 1 (characters) and Worksheet 2 (passages) for each learner. Alternatively, to save paper, either make the worksheets accessible in soft copy on learners' devices, or show them on a screen.

Introducing the exercise: Perhaps take one character, e.g. Mr. Grumpy, and ask the class how they think he usually speaks. Responses will probably relate to speed, low intonation, and a hoarse voice quality. Do not discourage nonverbal features, e.g. a grumpy facial expression.

Conducting the exercise: The worksheets contain:

- a list of *Mr. Men, Little Miss* characters. Their names are usually a clear indication of their personalities, e.g. Mr. Grumpy is always grumpy.
- a number of passages to be spoken.

Allocate each learner a character and one of the passages to read out. The rest of the class guess which character they are.

There is no problem if the same passage is allocated to more than one of the students/characters, e.g. Mr. Happy and Mr. Slow. This allows everyone to appreciate the differences between different speaking styles.

Debrief notes: Discuss with the learners the pronunciation features—mostly suprasegmentals—that they controlled to achieve the desired characters. For example, Mr. Forgetful is likely to use slower speed and plenty of pauses (and perhaps pause fillers, *um*s and *ah*s). Are the same features used when speaking in the learners' native languages?

Create your own materials: The full set of *Mr. Men, Little Miss* characters can be found at Mr. Men, Little Miss (2020), Wikipedia (n.d.). Some of them refer to non-language characteristics, e.g. Mr. Tall, Little Miss Neat, that cannot be used for pronunciation work.

Simply choose some more (suitable) characters, and produce more passages that can be pronounced in varying ways.

Worksheet 1

Your teacher will allocate you:

- one of the characters from the list
- one of the passages from the list

Practice and then read out the passage in the manner of the character.

Characters

Character	Personality
Little Miss **Busy**, or Mr. **Busy**	He/she can't sit still, but always has something to do, and is rushing around.
Little Miss **Careful**	She is cautious, and gives thought to things before she does them, to avoid accidents.
Mr. **Daydream**	He is always distracted by pleasant, faraway thoughts.
Little Miss **Fickle**	She has trouble making up her mind, and deciding what to do and what she likes.
Mr. **Forgetful**	He has a short memory, and can't remember facts and people, and what he was going to do.
Little Miss **Fun**	She loves to have fun all the time, and will do anything that is enjoyable or amusing.
Little Miss **Giggles**	Everything amuses her, so she can't stop giggling.
Mr. **Grumpy**, or Mr. **Miserable**	He is always unhappy, in a bad mood, hating anyone or anything he comes across.
Mr. **Happy**	He is positive and contented, finding pleasure in most things.
Little Miss **Loud**, or Mr. **Noisy**	He/she talks too much, usually in a very loud voice.
Little Miss **Naughty**, or Little Miss **Trouble**, or Mr. **Mischief**, or Mr. **Cheeky**	He/she loves to play practical jokes on anyone.
Little Miss **Quick**, or Mr. **Rush**	He/she never does anything properly, because he/she is always in a hurry.
Mr. **Rude**	He is impolite to everyone, and causes offense because of bad manners.
Little Miss **Shy**, or Mr. **Quiet**	He/she is afraid of everything, embarrassed or lacking in confidence.
Mr. **Slow**	He does everything very slowly, including speaking.
Little Miss **Stubborn**, or Mr. **Stubborn**	He/she always thinks he/she is right, even when other people have good ideas.
Mr. **Uppity**	He is very rich, feels he is better than others, and as a result is rude to everybody.
Mr. **Worry**	He is anxious about everything, whether it's real or not.

* This page is photocopiable for classroom use only.

Worksheet 2

1. I have a dog. Her name is Fifi. She's a poodle. She's white, and 12 years old. She used to play with me a lot, but now that she is getting older, she's happier just to sit on the sofa. I think she's getting a bit fat.
2. Would you like a coffee? They make very good coffee here. I think it's because of the beans they use. And coffee always goes well with a piece of cake. Would you like cake as well?
3. It was a memorable holiday. We arrived by plane, but our luggage went to Madrid! Fortunately our hotel provided us with a change of clothing until the luggage arrived. Then Mary got food poisoning. We think it was because of the prawns one evening.
4. I've got something to tell you. That house at the end of the street has been uninhabited for over two years now. I'm nervous every time I have to walk past it. It looks like it's something out of a horror movie.
5. I've started taking swimming lessons, because it's important that you should learn how to swim. My instructor's name is Helen, and she used to be a swimming champion. She's very good, and I'm already learning confidence in the water.
6. This has been a strange day. First of all, I woke up late. Then I couldn't find two matching socks, which is why I have odd ones on. Then, when I was halfway to school, I realized that I'd forgotten to comb my hair and it looked a real mess.
7. Shall we go shopping this Saturday? I really need a new pair of jeans, because my current pair are starting to look old. We could have a look at that new shop that's just opened: Glorious Jeans. They may have the kind of jeans I'm looking for.
8. Let me tell you about my boss. He's 75 years old, and has been in charge of the company for 37 years now. I'm not sure how much the company has changed in that time. But he wants to downsize now. I wonder when he'll retire.
9. Last summer, we went on holiday to Dubai. They have the #1 of everything: the world's tallest building, the world's first seven-star hotel, the world's largest shopping mall, and the world's largest performing fountain. It's strange to think that 40 years ago, it was all largely desert.
10. Graham has bought a new car. His old one was starting to look old and unloved. The paint was coming off in places, one wing mirror was hanging off, and it looked as though he had never actually washed it. I only hope he takes care of this new one.

* This page is photocopiable for classroom use only.

A5

Rhubarb

Pronunciation point: Rhubarb is the name of a plant that is eaten as a fruit, as in *rhubarb pie*. However, it is also *"British informal. The noise made by a group of actors to give the impression of indistinct background conversation, especially by the random repetition of the word 'rhubarb'"* (Lexico, n.d.). In other words, it is not the meaning of the word that is relevant, but the fact that it is produced with appropriate pronunciation to give the illusion of meaningful dialogue.

This exercise concentrates on suprasegmentals, and aims to produce dialogue that can be followed, even though there are no meaningful words.

Minimum level: Elementary

Exercise type: Pair dialogues, created by the learners

Approximate time: 5 minutes (preparation), 5 minutes (rehearsal), 20 minutes (exercise), 5 minutes (debrief)

Preparation: Make one copy of the worksheet for each learner. Alternatively, to save paper, either make the worksheet accessible in soft copy on learners' devices, or show the worksheet on a screen.

Introducing the exercise: This exercise follows nicely from the previous two. This exercise requires learners to use the same set of suprasegmentals to convey a dialogue in one given situation, using suprasegmentals and no meaningful words.

Conducting the exercise:

Divide the class into pairs, and give/show each learner the worksheet.

Tell each learner to think of a word of English. It could be simple words like the numbers one through ten, the colors, classroom words (*desk, chair, paper*, etc.). Short, simple words are preferable to longer, less common ones, like *rhubarb*, which may start to sound comical or difficult to pronounce when repeated.

Allocate each pair one of the scenarios. They should act out a one-minute scene, using only the words they have chosen. A role play could therefore go like this:

    A: Desk desk!
    B: Seven!
    A: Desk desk desk. Desk desk desk?
    B: Seven seven seven.
    A: Desk?
    B: Seven!

etc.

Learners should also be encouraged to use body language (facial expressions, gestures, etc.), since these features can perform a similar function to suprasegmentals.

Debrief notes: Discuss with the learners the pronunciation features—mostly suprasegmentals—that they controlled to achieve the desired emotions, status, etc.

Create your own materials: You do not need to write any dialogue. Simply create some scenarios. They should involve differences in status, and emotions such as fear, anger, sadness, joy, disgust, surprise, trust, anticipation.

Worksheet

Get into pairs.
    Each member should choose a simple word of English.
    Your pair will be allocated one of the scenarios below.
    Act out the scene, saying only the word you have chosen.

1. Two friends meet in a coffee bar. One tells the other a very funny joke. The other doesn't really understand the joke and asks for it to be explained. Of course, now it's not really funny anymore.

2. A car owner enters a repair shop because there is a strange knocking noise from the car's engine. The mechanic asks questions about what kind of noise it is, when it occurs, etc. The mechanic then quotes a price, and says it will take three days to fix. The owner is shocked at how much it will cost, and how long it will take.

3. A learner is rehearsing a speech they have to give in a foreign language. Their teacher keeps interrupting them because they are not loud enough, not expressive enough, showing too many nerves, etc.

4. Two work colleagues share an office. One asks the other to open the window because they are feeling hot and would like some fresh air. The other one says that opening the window makes the office noisy because there is a main road outside. The first one finally agrees and turns on a fan instead.

5. The receptionist at a doctor's clinic greets a new patient. Because they are new to the clinic, the receptionist has to enter the patient's details (name, address, telephone number, etc.) into the clinic's computer system, and check that it has been entered correctly, including the spelling.

6. A customer enters a shop with a faulty iron, disappointed because it was bought at the shop only last week. The shop assistant apologizes, calms the customer, takes the iron, writes down the customer's contact details, and promises that the manager will contact the customer the next day.

7. Two friends meet by accident at the airport. One has just returned from a group hiking holiday in the mountains and tells the other how magnificent it was. The other tells the story of when they were on a mountain trail last year, and another member of the group fell and twisted their ankle, and had to be air-lifted by helicopter.

* This page is photocopiable for classroom use only.

8 A teenager has had a tattoo, without their parents' knowledge. When they reveal this to their mother/father, the parent initially hates it, and tries to convince the teenager not to get another one. The teenager cannot understand all the fuss about a small tattoo.

9 A customer does the weekly shopping in a supermarket and takes it to the cashier. The cashier announces that, because they are the 100th customer today, they have won a prize: their shopping is free! The customer is delighted, and happily poses for photographs.

10 A manager is interviewing an applicant for a position. The manager asks about qualifications and experience, and the answers seem pleasing. But then the manager asks about willingness to work on Saturdays, and the applicant says they cannot. But surely this person read the job description in the advertisement?

* This page is photocopiable for classroom use only.

A6

Big and Small Mistakes

Pronunciation point: Not every feature of pronunciation is equally important. While they should all be mastered by any learner wanting to acquire a quasi-native pronunciation, for learners with lower aims, some are more important than others. Or, to put it another way, some features must be mastered because the consequences are more serious than for other features.

Minimum level: Intermediate

Exercise type: A form asking for learners' individual opinions, followed by discussion

Approximate time: 30 minutes (pre-teaching), 30 minutes (exercise), 20 minutes (debrief)

Preparation: Make one copy of the worksheet for each learner. Alternatively, to save paper, either make the worksheet accessible in soft copy on learners' devices, or show the worksheet on a screen.

Introducing the exercise: Explain that, just as in their own languages, some pronunciation features are more important than others.

Conducting the exercise: Give, or show, the learners the worksheet, and tell them to rank each feature on a five-point scale according to importance, where 1 = important and 5 = unimportant. You may need to go through all the features, in order to make sure that learners understand what is meant by each of them. Check that they are not putting "1" for every feature, as if everything is equally important! Emphasize that there are no "right" or "wrong" answers, and that the class will usually agree fairly well among themselves.

Debrief notes: The exercise is short for the learners to complete. What takes profitable time is the discussion in the debrief.

Ask the learners not only what rankings they gave, but also, and perhaps more importantly, why. Why are some features important/not important? Reasons given will probably relate to three questions:

1. Does this feature affect intelligibility because, for example, there are lots of words that are distinguished by these two sounds?
2. Is this feature associated with the image of a non-proficient speaker (and is therefore one that should be mastered)?
3. Is this a common feature of speakers from my country (and therefore something I might want to keep, as a marker of identity)?

The following responses (from Brown, 2000) were given by a group of international pronunciation experts:

#	Feature	Score
1	Unmarked sentence stress	1.25
2	Contrastive stress	1.52
3	Stress in multisyllable words	1.58
4	Pausing	1.67
5	Rhythm	1.70
6	Correcting stress	1.73
7	Stress in noun/verb pairs	2.15
8	Linking	2.15
9	Morphologically determined stress	2.15
10	Speed	2.18
11	Initial CC	2.24
12	Weak forms	2.27
13	Phonemic vowel length	2.30
14	Final CC	2.42
15	Allophonic vowel length	2.42
16	Proclaiming and referring tone	2.58
17	Initial CCC	2.59
18	Aspiration	2.64
19	Key	2.67
20	Loudness	2.78
21	All contrasting vowels	2.90
22	Final CCC	2.94
23	Spelling	3.00
24	Non-verbal features	3.14
25	Elision	3.33

26	The *th* sounds	3.36
27	Assimilation	3.55
28	Voice quality	3.77
29	Final CCCC	3.85

This does not mean that these are the "right" answers; merely, that this is what international experts thought. It may explain to you why this book is organized the way it is.

Worksheet

Below are 29 features of English pronunciation. They are not all equally important. If a learner of English does not pronounce these features correctly, how serious a problem do you feel this is? Rank each one from 1 (important) to 5 (unimportant).

Feature	Explanation, example	Ranking 1 = important 5 = unimportant
All contrasting vowels	Keeping all vowel sounds distinct.	
Allophonic vowel length	e.g. The vowel in *need* is longer than that in *neat*.	
Aspiration	There is a puff of air when you release the /p/ of *pit* that is not there in *bit*.	
Assimilation	*Great Britain* is usually pronounced *Grape Britain*.	
Contrastive stress	e.g. A: What are you doing? B: Nothing much. What are YOU doing?	
Correcting stress	e.g. A: 2018? B: No, Twenty NINEteen.	
Elision	e.g. The /t/ of *last week* is usually elided (dropped).	
Final CC	As in *grasp*.	
Final CCC	As in *plants*.	
Final CCCC	As in *texts* /teksts/.	
Initial CC	As in *star*.	
Initial CCC	As in *street*.	
Key	Among other things, key changes (a heightening or lowering of pitch range) are used in speech to show a change in topic or paragraph.	
Linking	Final sounds of words are linked to the initial sounds of following words, e.g. *bank account* and *banker count* become the same.	
Loudness	Not being too quiet or too loud.	
Morphologically determined stress	When endings are added to stems, the stress often moves within the stem, e.g. *PHOtograph, phoTOgraphy, photoGRAPHic*.	
Non-verbal features	Body language (gestures, facial expressions, etc.) accompanying speech.	
Pausing	Pausing in the right places.	

* This page is photocopiable for classroom use only.

Feature	Explanation, example	Ranking 1 = important 5 = unimportant
Phonemic vowel length	e.g. The vowel in *beat* is long, and that in *bit* is short.	
Proclaiming and referring tone	Proclaiming tone (a fall in many accents) marks new material that has not been mentioned before, while a referring tone (a fall-rise) marks given material.	
Rhythm	Stress-based timing, rather than syllable-based timing.	
Speed	Not speaking too quickly or too slowly.	
Spelling	Correspondences between letters and sounds.	
Stress in multisyllable words	*MediterRAnean* has stress on the fourth syllable (/reɪ/).	
Stress in noun/verb pairs	As a noun, *SUBject* has stress on the first syllable, but as a verb, it is on the second (*subJECT*).	
The *th* sounds	Pronouncing /θ, ð/ distinctly from /t, d, s, z, f, v/.	
Unmarked sentence stress	The lexical content words (nouns, verbs, adjectives, and adverbs) normally receive stress, while the grammatical function words do not.	
Voice quality	Such as overall tenseness, whisperiness, nasality.	
Weak forms	The vowels of grammatical function words are reduced to schwa or lost altogether, e.g. *to* /tə/.	

* This page is photocopiable for classroom use only.

A7

My Language or Yours?

Pronunciation point: All languages have their own phonology; that is, their own set of vowel and consonant sounds, suprasegmentals, voice quality, etc. English is not English words pronounced as if they were in the learners' native language (say, French) and, vice versa, French is not French words spoken as if they were English.

Minimum level: Elementary

Exercise type: A listening task, followed by discussion

Approximate time: 10 minutes (exercise), 10 minutes (debrief)

Preparation: The worksheets you use depend on the native languages of your learners. Four exercises are given for German, Turkish, Malay, and Thai. However, teachers should prepare similar worksheets for the particular languages of their learners. This requires a reasonable understanding of the pronunciation features, and typical mistakes, of the learners.

Make one copy of the worksheet for each learner. Alternatively, to save paper, either make the worksheet accessible in soft copy on learners' devices, or show the worksheet on a screen.

Introducing the exercise: If you have French or German learners, you could begin with a bit of light relief: the following transliterations of the English *Humpty Dumpty* rhyme into French and German spelling (Hulme, 1981; van Rooten, 1967). They are mostly nonsense in those languages.

English	French	German
Humpty Dumpty	Un petit d'un petit	Um die Dumm' die
Sat on a wall.	S'étonne aux Halles	Saturn Aval;
Humpty Dumpty	Un petit d'un petit	Um die Dumm' die
Had a great fall.	Ah! degrés te fallent	Ader Grät fahl.
And all the king's horses	Indolent qui ne sort cesse	Alter ging's Ohr sass
And all the king's men	Indolent qui ne se mène	und Alter ging's mähen
Couldn't put Humpty	Qu'importe un petit	Kuh den "putt" um Dieter
Together again.	Tout gai de Reguennes.	Gitter er gähn.

Conducting the exercise: Learners listen to a speaker read out one of the words. The speaker may be a live speaker (that is, the teacher or a guest) or a recording. They decide (i) whether it is the first or second language, and (ii) what features of the pronunciation led to that answer.

As a variation, the teacher could ask the learners to choose either the English word or the other one, and say it out loud. The teacher then guesses which word was being pronounced.

Debrief notes:

Although it has been influenced by many languages in its history, English is considered a Germanic language, dating back to the invasion in the 5th century of tribes (mainly the Angles, Saxons, and Jutes) from present-day northern Germany (and parts of Denmark and the Netherlands). For this reason, the differences between present-day English and German are relatively small. At the other extreme, English and Thai are unrelated, so the differences are large.

Many words have been borrowed from English into other languages, usually with regularization in terms of conforming to the borrowing language's phonology and spelling system. This has had the result that the same original word (*restaurant, taxi, telephone*, etc.) is pronounced in two slightly different ways, highlighting the differences between the phonologies of the two languages.

The features of the sound systems of the two languages that allow the learners to identify the language may be of various kinds, such as the following:

- The way sounds are typically pronounced, for instance:
    - the post-alveolar /r/ of English versus the uvular /r/ of German
    - the syllable-final /r/ of English (a voiced approximant), if pronounced, versus that of Turkish (a devoiced (voiceless) fricative)

- Differences in the typical amount of aspiration of plosives; that is, the /ʰ/ in English *tuck* /tʰʌk/ versus Malay *tak*
- Nuances of vowel quality
- The tendency for vowels to be diphthongized, e.g. whether /eə/ is pronounced as a diphthong /eə/ or as a long monophthong /ɛ:/
- Differences in the amount of lip rounding
- Differences in possible sounds in syllable positions, for instance:
    - whether syllable-initial and/or syllable-final consonant clusters are permissible
    - whether /r/ can occur in syllable-final position (rhoticity)
    - whether /h/ is a syllable-final possibility
    - devoicing of final sounds, e.g. English *vague* with /g/ versus German *Weg* with /k/
- A large or small difference between stressed and unstressed syllables
- Speed of utterance
- Thai is a tonal language, while English is not

Create your own materials: A worksheet using English and another language can easily be produced, but requires an in-depth knowledge of the phonology of the other language, and a native or native-like pronunciation of both languages.

Worksheet (German)

Your instructor will say or play a recording of one word from each line, either the English word or the German word. You need to listen carefully and tick whether you think it was the English or German word.

#	English	German	German meaning
1	❏ *bright*	❏ *breit*	"wide"
2	❏ *fear*	❏ *vier*	"four"
3	❏ *air*	❏ *er*	"he"
4	❏ *gross*	❏ *groß*	"large"
5	❏ *dust*	❏ *dass*	"that"
6	❏ *knee*	❏ *nie*	"never"
7	❏ *my*	❏ *Mai*	"May"
8	❏ *zoo*	❏ *zu*	"to"
9	❏ *hunt*	❏ *Hand*	"hand"
10	❏ *boiler*	❏ *Beule*	"bump"
11	❏ *stark*	❏ *stark*	"strong"
12	❏ *tile*	❏ *Teil*	"part"
13	❏ *feel*	❏ *viel*	"much"
14	❏ *vague*	❏ *Weg*	"way"
15	❏ *vice*	❏ *weiß*	"white"
16	❏ *done*	❏ *dann*	"then"
17	❏ *felt*	❏ *Feld*	"field"
18	❏ *nine*	❏ *nein*	"no"
19	❏ *common*	❏ *kommen*	"come"
20	❏ *mention*	❏ *Menschen*	"people"

* This page is photocopiable for classroom use only.

Worksheet (Turkish)

Your instructor will say or play a recording of one word from each line, either the English word or the Turkish word. You need to listen carefully and tick whether you think it was the English or Turkish word.

#	English	Turkish	Turkish meaning
1	❏ on	❏ on	"ten"
2	❏ sue	❏ su	"water"
3	❏ her	❏ her	"each"
4	❏ buy	❏ bay	"Mr."
5	❏ more	❏ mor	"purple"
6	❏ yield	❏ yıl	"year"
7	❏ doctor	❏ doktor	"doctor"
8	❏ honor	❏ ona	"her"
9	❏ air	❏ eğer	"if"
10	❏ taxi	❏ taksi	"taxi"
11	❏ higher	❏ hayır	"no"
12	❏ Kim	❏ kim	"who"
13	❏ shoe	❏ şu	"that"
14	❏ Fiat	❏ fiyat	"price"
15	❏ booze	❏ buz	"ice"
16	❏ Adam	❏ adam	"man"
17	❏ beer	❏ bir	"one"
18	❏ Benny	❏ beni	"me"
19	❏ service	❏ ceviz	"walnut"
20	❏ Nissan	❏ Nisan	"April"

* This page is photocopiable for classroom use only.

Worksheet (Malay)

Your instructor will say or play a recording of one word from each line, either the English word or the Malay word. You need to listen carefully and tick whether you think it was the English or Malay word.

#	English	Malay	Malay meaning
1	❑ *hurry*	❑ *hari*	"day"
2	❑ *cow*	❑ *kau*	"you"
3	❑ *Dan*	❑ *dan*	"and"
4	❑ *tuck*	❑ *tak*	"not"
5	❑ *line*	❑ *lain*	"other"
6	❑ *dear*	❑ *dia*	"he, she"
7	❑ *llama*	❑ *lama*	"old"
8	❑ *young*	❑ *yang*	"which"
9	❑ *lucky*	❑ *laki*	"man"
10	❑ *bike*	❑ *baik*	"good"
11	❑ *jam*	❑ *jam*	"hour"
12	❑ *Murray*	❑ *mari*	"come"
13	❑ *summer*	❑ *sama*	"same"
14	❑ *rumor*	❑ *rumah*	"house"
15	❑ *knack*	❑ *nak*	"want"
16	❑ *cutter*	❑ *kata*	"word"
17	❑ *suck it*	❑ *sakit*	"pain"
18	❑ *under*	❑ *anda*	"you"
19	❑ (Cornish) *pasty*	❑ *pasti*	"sure"
20	❑ *quota*	❑ *kota*	"city"

* This page is photocopiable for classroom use only.

Worksheet (Thai)

Your instructor will say or play a recording of one word from each line, either the English word or the Thai word. You need to listen carefully and tick whether you think it was the English or Thai word.

#	English	Thai	Phonemic transcription	Thai meaning
1	❑ D	❑ ดี	/dii/	"good"
2	❑ cow	❑ เขา	/khau/	"he"
3	❑ one	❑ วัน	/wan/	"day"
4	❑ jet	❑ เจ็ด	/cèt/	"seven"
5	❑ crew	❑ ครู	/khruu/	"teacher"
6	❑ bee	❑ ปี	/pii/	"year"
7	❑ Ma	❑ มา	/maa/	"come"
8	❑ paw	❑ พอ	/phɔɔ/	"enough"
9	❑ me	❑ มี	/mii/	"have"
10	❑ pen	❑ เป็น	/pen/	"be"
11	❑ cry	❑ ใคร	/khrai/	"who"
12	❑ soon	❑ ศูนย์	/sǔun/	"zero"
13	❑ guy	❑ ไก่	/kài/	"chicken"
14	❑ bit	❑ ปิด	/pìt/	"shut"
15	❑ hen	❑ เห็น	/hěn/	"see"
16	❑ long	❑ ลง	/loŋ/	"down"
17	❑ high	❑ ให้	/hâi/	"give"
18	❑ sea	❑ สี่	/sìi/	"four"
19	❑ sway	❑ สวย	/sǔai/	"beautiful"
20	❑ nutty	❑ นาที	/naathii/	"minute"

* This page is photocopiable for classroom use only.

A8

English With My Native Voice Quality, My Native Language With English Voice Quality

Pronunciation point: As should have become obvious in the previous exercise, the phonology of a language is composed of many features. They all go together and interact to give the overall "feel" of the language. In everyday language, the term *voice quality* is often used for this, although it has a more specific meaning in phonetics. One writer (Honikman, 1964) told her learners to "get into gear" for speaking English; that is, abandon the long-term settings of their native language and switch to those of English. An 11-year-old learner (quoted by Laroy, 1995, p. 35), upon being asked, "How come you suddenly pronounce English so well?" replied, "I am making fun of them when they speak our language."

Minimum level: Elementary

Exercise type: A production exercise

Approximate time: 10 minutes (exercise), 10 minutes (debrief)

Preparation: Make a copy of the worksheet (or any other alternative passage) for each learner. Alternatively, to save paper, show it on a screen.

Introducing the exercise:

Ask the learners how their native language sounds when an English speaker pronounces it poorly. Most learners probably have experience of English speakers trying to learn their language, and sounding like an English speaker trying to learn their language; that is, speaking their language, but with English vowel and consonant sounds, English stress, English intonation, etc.

This question will probably lead to an amusing few minutes of learners showing how badly some English speakers speak their language. However, it may lead to exaggerated Englishness, and pronunciation features that are caricatures of English speakers, and not the way English speakers actually pronounce things.

An example of this kind of exaggeration is the French accent adopted by Peter Sellers in the *Pink Panther* films. Planchenault (2015) gives some examples (from *The Pink Panther Strikes Again*, 1976):

"This is Inspector Clouseau [klyzœ] speaking on the phone [fœn]."
"Do you have a room [rym]?"
"Does your dog bite [ba:t]?"

[y] is like the vowel of *beat*, but with lip-rounding. Similarly, [œ] is like the vowel of *bet*, but with lip-rounding. There is no reason why Clouseau, being after all French, cannot pronounce his name the French way [kluzo] (nor [fon], [rum] or [baɪt]). This exaggerated mispronunciation was adopted by Steve Martin in the remakes (2006, 2009). It has produced a few scholarly articles, e.g. Pickett (2004).

A similarly comical pronunciation may be familiar to readers from Office Crabtree of the *'Allo 'Allo* TV series, with two differences: this is an Englishman pretending to be French and mispronouncing English, and the mispronunciations seem more like misspellings:

"The British Air Farce have dropped their bums on the water works. They have scored a direct hot on the pimps" (*Force, bombs, hit, pumps*)

Again, this may be amusing (and has spawned *Officer Crabtree's Fronch phrose berk*; Bostrom, 2018), but it is not accurate interlanguage, although it was said to be based on the pronunciation of 1970s British prime minister Edward Heath, who spoke French fluently but with a clear English accent (Allo Allo Wiki, n.d.).

So, what the original question "How does your language sound when pronounced not very well by an English speaker?" tries to elicit is not caricatures, but more accurate performances.

Conducting the exercise:

Part 1

Give the learners a copy of the worksheet. Two worksheets are provided here, one for AmE teaching environments, one for BrE. Alternatively, to save paper, show it on a screen. Ask the learners how a native speaker of their language would pronounce it.

Any alternative English passage that the learners are familiar with could be used.

Ask the learners to identify the pronunciation features that make it sound non-English. Compile a list on the whiteboard, flipchart, etc.; these are the features that the learners should try to avoid if they want to sound like a native speaker of English.

Part 2

Ask the learners to recite the words of their countries' national anthem (or any other alternative passage), but the way an (American or British) English speaker would read them. Ask the learners to identify the pronunciation features that make it sound English. Compile a list on the whiteboard, flipchart, etc.; these are the features that the learners should try to adopt if they want to sound like a native speaker of English.

Debrief notes: Notice that, in exercise A1, we saw that not all learners necessarily want or need to acquire a native speaker accent of English.

Worksheet (AmE)

Here are the words of the American national anthem.
How would a typical speaker of your native language pronounce it?

US National Anthem

Oh, say can you see,
By the dawn's early light,
What so proudly we hailed
At the twilight's last gleaming?

Whose broad stripes and bright stars,
Through the perilous fight,
O'er the ramparts we watched,
Were so gallantly streaming?

And the rockets' red glare,
The bombs bursting in air,
Gave proof through the night
That our flag was still there.

O say, does that star-spangled
Banner yet wave
O'er the land of the free
And the home of the brave?

* This page is photocopiable for classroom use only.

Worksheet (BrE)

Here are the words of the British national anthem.
How would a typical speaker of your native language pronounce it?

UK National Anthem

God save our gracious Queen,
Long live our noble Queen,
God save the Queen!
Send her victorious,
Happy and glorious,
Long to reign over us,
God save the Queen!

* This page is photocopiable for classroom use only.

Section B
Suprasegmentals

B1
Waking Up for Class

Pronunciation point: Raps are a popular and fun way to practice suprasegmentals, especially stress placement and the weakening of unstressed syllables. In order to fit unstressed syllables between the very regular stressed syllables, they need to be weakened and shortened (called the concertina effect by Abercrombie, 1967, p. 97).

Since the words are spoken rather than sung, raps are ideal for students who cannot sing in tune.

Minimum level: Elementary

Exercise type: A rap, best performed as a class

Approximate time: 15 minutes (exercise)

Preparation: Make one copy of the worksheet for each learner. Alternatively, to save paper, either make the worksheet accessible in soft copy on learners' devices, or show the worksheet on a screen.

Introducing the exercise: All students will surely know what a rap is. Point out the strict regularity of the beat, and that the words therefore have to be fitted into that beat. Some devices for achieving that are shown in the spelling (*gonna, gotta, wanna*).

Explain some language points:

- *the crack of dawn* is a set phrase for "daybreak."
- (for BrE speakers) *drapes* are curtains.
- *sec* is short for *second*.
- *Too much speed, not enough haste* refers to the expression *more haste, less speed*, meaning doing something in too much of a hurry.
- *Zzzzzzz* is a way of showing sleep, including perhaps snoring, in writing.

Conducting the exercise: A steady beat needs to be established. One fun way of doing this is to get the students to produce it in the manner of Queen's "We Will Rock You": namely, two slaps on the thighs followed by one clap in the air.

The first time, this beat can be fairly slow as the students get used to the words and stress placement of the passage. In subsequent times, the beat can be quickened.

Two versions of the rap are given. The left-hand version is in normal spelling. In the right-hand version, the syllables to be stressed are shown in capital letters; this may help learners initially. Some variation in the placement of stress is possible. As learners get used to the text, they can use the left-hand version more.

Debrief notes: Draw learners' attention to aspects of connected speech:

- weak forms (e.g. /əv/ not /ɒv/)
- elision (e.g. possible loss of /v/ in *slice of bread*)
- assimilation (e.g. *don't care* /doʊŋk ker/ (AmE) ~ /dəʊŋk keə/ (BrE))
- linking (shown by *gotta*, etc.; (for BrE speakers) /r/ in *quarter of*)

These are all perfectly normal in faster, colloquial speech.

Create your own materials: You can, of course, use actual raps.

To create your own:

- decide on the topic
- find rhyming words connected to that topic; there are plenty of rhyming dictionaries on the internet
- write the verses with four beats in each line

Worksheet

I slowly yawn, it's the crack of dawn	i SLOWly YAWN, it's the CRACK of DAWN
Gotta get up, see the drapes are drawn	GOTta get UP, see the DRAPES are DRAWN
Get out of bed, my eyes are red	GET out of BED, my EYES are RED
Gotta get ready for the day ahead	GOTta get READy for the DAY aHEAD
Take a quick shower, a really cold shower	TAKE a quick SHOWER, a REALly cold SHOWER
Gotta get going in a quarter of an hour	GOTta get GOing in a QUARTer of an HOUR
Comb my hair, choose what to wear	COMB my HAIR, CHOOSE what to WEAR
Don' wanna look like I just don't care	DON' wanna LOOK like i JUST don't CARE
Quickly get dressed, gotta look my best	QUICKly get DRESSED, gotta LOOK my BEST
Gonna make sure my teacher's impressed	GONna make SURE my TEACHer's imPRESSED
Have a slice of bread, though I feel half-dead	HAVE a slice of BREAD, though i FEEL half-DEAD
Don' want tea, I'll have coffee instead	DON' want TEA, i'll have COFfee inSTEAD
Got a grammar test, that's why I'm stressed	GOT a grammar TEST, that's WHY I'm STRESSED
It's how our English skills are assessed	it's HOW our ENGlish SKILLS are asSESSED
But wait a sec, let me check	but WAIT a SEC, LET me CHECK
I'm all disorganized. What the heck!	i'm ALL disORGanized. WHAT the HECK!
Today's not Monday, this is Sunday!	ToDAY'S not MONday, THIS is SUNday!
Aaargh! I've got the dates wrong by one day	AAARGH! i've GOT the dates WRONG by ONE day
What a waste, I shouldn't have raced	WHAT a WASTE, i SHOULDn't have RACED
Too much speed, not enough haste	TOO much SPEED, NOT enough HASTE
Go back to bed, my eyes still red	GO back to BED, my EYES still RED
There's a noisy pounding in my head	there's a NOISy POUNDing IN my HEAD
I wanna just weep, go back to sleep	i WANna just WEEP, GO back to SLEEP
One two three four, counting sheep	ONE two THREE four, COUNTing SHEEP
Zzzzzzz	*Zzzzzzz*

* This page is photocopiable for classroom use only.

Waking Up for Class ◆ 57

B2
There Was a Young Lady From . . .

Pronunciation point: Stresses are important in English, as are the processes that accompany them. The ends of the lines in limericks (and other poems) rhyme. This means that the sounds from the vowel of the stressed syllable of the final words are the same (or very similar).

As for the title of this exercise, many limericks start *There was a young lady from* [place name]. A number can be found on the internet. But beware: they are sometimes a bit racy or downright obscene, so not suitable for the classroom.

Minimum level: Intermediate

Exercise type: A paper exercise for students working in pairs, followed by pronunciation practice

Approximate time: 10 minutes (introducing the limerick format), 20 minutes (exercise), 10 minutes (debrief)

Preparation: Make one copy of Worksheet A, and one copy of Worksheet B for each pair of students (e.g. in a class of 20, make ten copies of each worksheet).

Introducing the exercise: Introduce the limerick poetic format, using the following limerick:

> Archimedes, the well-known truth-seeker,
> Jumping out of his bath, cried, "Eureka!"
> He ran half a mile,
> Wearing only a smile,
> And became the world's very first streaker.

Explain and illustrate the characteristics of the limerick:

- It is humorous.
- It is written as five lines.

- The first, second, and last lines rhyme (*seeker, Eureka,* and *streaker*), as do the third and fourth lines (*mile* and *smile*). *Rhyme* means that the sounds from the stressed syllables of the words onwards are the same or very similar (/iːkə(r)/).
- The first, second and last lines have three stresses each (*-me-, well,* and *seek-; out, bath,* and *-re-;* and *-came, ve-,* and *streak-*), while the third and fourth lines have two each (*ran* and *mile; on-* and *smile*).
- The first, second, and last lines each have an extra beat (a silent stress) at the end. It is not natural to continue from *seeker* straight into *jumping*.
- Thus, the limerick is pronounced as follows (with the extra beat shown by Δ):

  archiMEdes, the WELL-known truth-SEEKer Δ
  jumping OUT of his BATH, cried, "euREka!" Δ
  he RAN half a MILE
  wearing ONly a SMILE,
  and beCAME the world's VEry first STREAKer. Δ

- This is, in fact, a very regular poetical form. If we combined the third and fourth lines, we would end up with four lines, each with four beats.
- It is also regular in that the rhythm is usually a stressed syllable followed by two unstressed syllables, as in *ME—des—the, WELL—known—truth*.

Practice reading this limerick with the students, until you are sure they understand the format.

Conducting the exercise:

1. This game should be played in pairs.
2. Give one member of each pair Worksheet A, and the other Worksheet B.
3. Explain that the worksheets contain all the lines of eight limericks, but they have been jumbled and split between the two worksheets. However, the lines are shown in their right position, i.e. first lines are printed as first lines, etc.
4. The pair have to reassemble the eight limericks. They must not look at each other's worksheets, but should ask questions like, "Do you have a line that rhymes with *took*?"
5. When the students have got the right answers, practice reading the limericks out loud.

Create your own materials: There are plenty of websites with limericks. However, some of them are not proper limericks, in that they do not follow the structure outlined above.

You can, of course, use poems that are not limericks, but nevertheless have end-of-line rhyme.

Answer

There was a young lady named Harris,
Whom nothing could ever embarrass,
'Til the salts that she shook
In the bath that she took,
Turned out to be Plaster of Paris.

There was a young man from Darjeeling,
Who got on the bus for West Ealing.
It said on the door
"Don't spit on the floor,"
So he stood up and spat on the ceiling.

There was an old barn owl named Boo,
Who used, every night, to yell, "Hoo."
A kid once walked by,
And started to cry,
And called out, "I haven't a clue!"

There was a young man from Hong Kong,
Who wrote a new popular song.
But the song that he wrote
Was all on one note,
Though it sounded superb on a gong.

I'm papering walls in the loo,
And frankly I haven't a clue.
For the pattern's all wrong,
Or the paper's too long,
And I'm stuck to the toilet with glue.

I'd rather have fingers than toes.
I'd rather have ears than a nose.
And as for my hair,
I'm glad it's all there.
I'll be awfully sad when it goes.

There once was a slimmer named Green,
Who grew so incredibly lean,
And flat, and compressed,
That his back touched his chest,
So that sideways he couldn't be seen.

There was a young schoolboy of Rye,
Who was baked by mistake in a pie.
To his mother's disgust,
He emerged through the crust,
And exclaimed, with a yawn, "Where am I?"

Worksheet A

There was a young lady named Harris
Who was baked by mistake in a pie.
It said on the door
I'm glad it's all there.
And called out, "I haven't a clue!"

There was a young man from Darjeeling,
Who grew so incredibly lean,
A kid once walked by,
Or the paper's too long,
Turned out to be Plaster of Paris.

There was an old barn owl named Boo,
And frankly I haven't a clue.
But the song that he wrote
He emerged through the crust,
Though it sounded superb on a gong.

There was a young man from Hong Kong,
I'd rather have ears than a nose.
'Til the salts that she shook
That his back touched his chest,
So he stood up and spat on the ceiling.

* This page is photocopiable for classroom use only.

Worksheet B

I'm papering walls in the loo*,
Who got on the bus for West Ealing.
And as for my hair,
In the bath that she took,
And exclaimed, with a yawn, "Where am I?"

* *loo*: BrE for "toilet"

I'd rather have fingers than toes.
Who wrote a new popular song.
To his mother's disgust,
And started to cry,
So that sideways he couldn't be seen.

There once was a slimmer named Green,
Whom nothing could ever embarrass,
For the pattern's all wrong,
"Don't spit on the floor,"
And I'm stuck to the toilet with glue.

There was a young schoolboy of Rye,
Who used, every night, to yell, "Hoo."
And flat, and compressed,
Was all on one note,
I'll be awfully sad when it goes.

* This page is photocopiable for classroom use only.

B3

And to End the News, . . .

Pronunciation point: Paragraphs are used in writing to show where the writer is starting a new topic. These changes in topic are also signaled in pronunciation. A change of paragraph is usually signaled by:

- a long pause between the paragraphs
- ending the previous paragraph with a lowered pitch and reduced loudness
- starting the new paragraph with a heightened pitch and increased loudness

This is known in academic phonetics as *key* (see Bradford, 1988; Brazil, 1997; Brazil, Coulthard & Johns, 1980; Wells, 2006).

Minimum level: Intermediate

Exercise type: Analysis of a text, then speaking out loud, individually

Approximate time: 10 minutes (inserting paragraph breaks), 15 minutes (reading aloud), 5 minutes (debrief)

Preparation: Make one copy of the worksheet for each learner. Alternatively, to save paper, either make the worksheet accessible in soft copy on learners' devices, or show the worksheet on a screen.

Introducing the exercise: Ask the students what they know about paragraphs in writing (in English, and probably in their own language too). Elicit the idea of a change of topic.

Conducting the exercise: Distribute the worksheet, or show it on screen. Explain that it has been printed without any paragraph breaks. Instruct the learners to mark where paragraph breaks should occur in the written form. Once a consensus has been reached, ask the learners how they think these paragraph breaks should be signaled in the pronunciation. Get learners to read the passage out loud, to each other or to the class.

Answers: Here is the passage with paragraph breaks shown.

> And to end the news, here are the main points again.
>
> The prime minister has completed his official visit to Canada. He said that he had had productive discussions with Canadian officials on a possible free trade agreement, and hoped this would make possible increased two-way trade between the countries. He is accompanied by his wife, and representatives of the Ministry of Trade. He now continues to the USA, the next stop on his one-week tour.
>
> The Ministry of Labor has just released official statistics indicating that productivity has risen by the largest jump in the last eight years. The increase of 1.3% recorded between July and December this year was caused in part by increased automation, and changes in working practices. However, the government has warned that this increase is unlikely to continue into the new year.
>
> In the latest round of mid-week league matches, East Shore United have beaten Wellington Rangers 4–1, to take a five-point lead at the top of the table. Their nearest rivals, Hamilton United, were held to a 1–1 draw at home by Epsom Rovers. The two teams meet in a top-of-the-table clash on Saturday.
>
> Two unconnected multiple-car crashes on the Northwest Highway have left three people dead and nine in hospital. The Traffic Police have stated that the accidents were caused by drivers not making adequate allowances for the foggy conditions this morning. They remind drivers to turn on headlights and to slow down when it is foggy.
>
> And that's the end of the news.

Debriefing note: Point out how the pronunciation equivalent of paragraph breaks entails leaving sizeable pauses between them. Pausing is the subject of another exercise in this section.

Create your own materials: This exercise is easy to create. Simply take a suitable passage and rewrite it without paragraph breaks. This means that:

- you should use a passage at an appropriate level (of grammar, vocabulary, etc.) for the learners.
- the passage can be one that has already been used in class.
- the passage should not be so short that there will be no paragraph breaks, or that each paragraph will only be a sentence or two.
- the passage should not be so long that each paragraph is long, and the passage takes a while to read.
- the passage should have clear changes in topic.

- paragraph breaks may also signal a change of speaker. So, you could use a dialogue.
- you should take out the paragraph breaks, but keep all other punctuation (full-stops, commas, capital letters, etc.), unlike in the pauses exercise in this section (B8).

Worksheet

Here is the word-for-word transcript of a radio news broadcast. Read through it and mark where you think the newsreader's script had new paragraphs.

> And to end the news, here are the main points again. The prime minister has completed his official visit to Canada. He said that he had had productive discussions with Canadian officials on a possible free trade agreement, and hoped this would make possible increased two-way trade between the countries. He is accompanied by his wife, and representatives of the Ministry of Trade. He now continues to the USA, the next stop on his one-week tour. The Ministry of Labor has just released official statistics indicating that productivity has risen by the largest jump in the last eight years. The increase of 1.3% recorded between July and December this year was caused in part by increased automation, and changes in working practices. However, the government has warned that this increase is unlikely to continue into the new year. In the latest round of mid-week league matches, East Shore United have beaten Wellington Rangers 4–1, to take a five-point lead at the top of the table. Their nearest rivals, Hamilton United, were held to a 1–1 draw at home by Epsom Rovers. The two teams meet in a top-of-the-table clash on Saturday. Two unconnected multiple-car crashes on the Northwest Highway have left three people dead and nine in hospital. The Traffic Police have stated that the accidents were caused by drivers not making adequate allowances for the foggy conditions this morning. They remind drivers to turn on headlights and to slow down when it is foggy. And that's the end of the news.

Obviously, if you are reading out the news, your audience can't see the paragraph breaks in your script. How do you think the newsreader should convey this information in his or her pronunciation?

* This page is photocopiable for classroom use only.

B4

My Name's Sophie

Pronunciation point: New information, including contrast, is a very strong element in pronunciation. New items are given the main stress (on the stressed syllable of the word, if it is multisyllabic). Thus, if student 1 asks, "How did David do in English?" student 2's reply, "He scored an *A* in English," will place the stress on *A*, because that is the new information (while *English* is given, i.e. already mentioned). However, if student 1 asks, "Did David score any A grades?" the answer will be, "He scored an A in ENglish," since *English* is now the new information, the answer to the question (while *A* is given).

Similarly, if student 1 asks, "Is this Victoria Street?" the response will be, No, THAT'S Victoria Street," as the contrast is between *this* and *that* (while *Victoria* remains constant, i.e. given). But if student 1 asks, "Is that Albert Street?" the answer will be, "No, that's VicTORia Street," because the contrast is now between *Albert* and *Victoria* (while *that* now remains constant).

Minimum level: Elementary

Exercise type: A production exercise to be completed in pairs. The learners have a choice over using stimulus sentences a or b.

Approximate time: 10 minutes (exercise), 10 minutes (debrief)

Preparation: Make one copy of Worksheet A and one copy of Worksheet B for each pair of students (e.g. in a class of 20, make ten copies of each worksheet).

Introducing the exercise: Explain that the way you say (stress) something depends on the context. Give an example:

"What's your name?" "My name's SOphie."
"Is her name Sophie?" "No, MY name's Sophie."

Conducting the exercise: Distribute the worksheets, A to one member of a pair, B to the other member. They must not look at each other's sheets.

Explain that in each of the following examples, sentence c could follow sentence a or b. However, if it follows a, it will be pronounced in a different way than if it follows b. Student A chooses either sentence a or b from their worksheet. Student B then responds with sentence c, but pronounced with the stress on the item that is appropriate in the context. Then the roles are reversed for the second example.

Create your own materials:

1. Write a response sentence that contains at least two potential major pieces of information, for instance, "I like swimming too."
2. Compose stimulus sentences that focus on one or other of the major pieces of information in the response, e.g. "I hear your wife likes swimming" (the response stresses *I*), "I hear you like boating" (the response stresses *SWIMming*).

Worksheet A

1. a How did David do in English?
   b Did David score any A grades?

2. c She's always unprepared.

3. a I hear your daughter has graduated from Oxford.
   b I hear your son has graduated from Cambridge.

4. c No, that's Victoria Street.

5. a I don't just dislike chilli, ...
   b I don't hate garlic, ...

6. c I completed my homework yesterday.

7. a At what time is your Geography lesson?
   b Why didn't you attend the meeting at 10?

8. c I don't like math.

9. a If only I could find last semester's Chemistry notes, ...
   b It's a bit inconvenient for you to take my notes because I really need them myself, but I suppose ...

10. c I'll start on the Physics assignment once I've finished the History assignment.

* This page is photocopiable for classroom use only.

Worksheet B

1 c He scored an A in English.

2 a Is she ever unprepared?
  b She leaves everything to the last minute, and as a result, . . .

3 c No, my daughter has graduated from Cambridge.

4 a Is this Victoria Street?
  b Is that Albert Street?

5 c I hate chilli.

6 a Have you completed your homework?
  b Why weren't you at the match yesterday?

7 c I've got Geography at 10.

8 a When did you realize you liked math?
  b I'd never work in a bank, because . . .

9 c I could make a copy of them for you.

10 a When will you start working on the Physics assignment?
   b What's next, after the History assignment?

* This page is photocopiable for classroom use only.

B5

What Year? Every Year

Pronunciation point: As in the previous exercises, pausing and stress are important in speech. Jokes often depend on contrast, and stress is used to bring out these contrasts.

Minimum level: Intermediate

Exercise type: Individual learner production of passages (jokes)

Approximate time: 5 minutes (preparation), 20 minutes (exercise), 10 minutes (debrief)

Preparation: Make one copy of the worksheet for each learner. Alternatively, to save paper, either make the worksheet accessible in soft copy on learners' devices, or show the worksheet on a screen.

Introducing the exercise: If you have not already completed the preceding exercises in this section, use the first joke. In the first line, *what, date,* and *birth* are the important words to be stressed. In the second, *July* and *sixteenth*; indeed, some people say "July sixteenth," showing that *the* is not important. In the third, *year*. In the fourth, *every* (and not *year*, because that was introduced in the third line).

Conducting the exercise: Learners can work individually, in pairs, or small groups.

1. They read the passages, highlighting the words that are important in terms of meaning and message, for instance by underlining.
2. They read the passages out loud, making sure they put stress on those underlined words, and leaving appropriate pauses.

Create your own materials: Jokes are useful in the language classroom, firstly because they are fun, and secondly because it now means that the learners know a joke in a foreign language. There are many joke websites on the internet, and publications like *Reader's Digest* contain suitable short jokes. Pick those jokes that involve a clear contrast, and thus an appropriate stress placement.

Worksheet

Passage 1

Q: What is your date of birth?
A: July the sixteenth.
Q: What year?
A: Every year.

Passage 2

Heaven is where the police are British, the chefs are Italian, the mechanics are German, the lovers are French, and it's all organized by the Swiss. Hell is where the police are German, the chefs are British, the mechanics are French, the lovers are Swiss, and it's all organized by the Italians!

Passage 3

One day, a little girl was sitting, watching her mother do the dishes at the kitchen sink. She suddenly noticed that her mother had several white hairs, sticking out in contrast on her dark brown head. She looked at her mother, and asked, "Why are some of your hairs white, Mum?"

Her mother replied, "Well, every time that you do something wrong, and you make me cry or unhappy, one of my hairs turns white."

The little girl thought about this for a while, and then asked, "Mummy, how come all of Grandma's hairs are white?"

Passage 4

A man was sitting at the bar staring at his drink, when a large, trouble-making motorbiker stepped up next to him, grabbed his drink, and finished it in one go.

"Well, whatcha gonna do about it?" he said, threateningly.

"This is the worst day of my life," the man said. "I'm a complete failure. I was late to a meeting and my boss fired me. When I went to the parking lot, I found my car had been stolen, and I don't have any insurance. I left my wallet in the cab I took home. Then, when I got home, my dog bit me. So I came to this bar to work up the courage to kill myself. I bought a drink, I dropped a capsule in it, and just sat here watching the poison dissolve. Then you showed up and drank the whole thing! But enough about me, how's your day going?"

* This page is photocopiable for classroom use only.

Passage 5

One day, a rich father decided to take his son to the countryside, to show him how poor some people are—in contrast to them, who live in a nice house in the wealthy suburbs of a big city. This way, his son could understand the value of things, and how lucky he is. So they went to the countryside, and spent one day and one night, in a simple countryside home.

On the journey back home, the father asked his son, "So, what did you think of this little trip?"

"It was great, Dad!"

"Did you see how poor some people are?"

"Yes. I saw that we have one dog; they have four. We have a pool at home; they live by a beautiful lake. The streetlamps give us light in our garden, whereas they get the light of a million stars. Our back yard ends at the fence; theirs is as far as the eye can see. And finally, I saw they had the time to talk to each other and live like a happy family; you and Mum work all day and I barely see you. Thanks, Dad, for showing me how rich we could be."

* This page is photocopiable for classroom use only.

B6

What's the Difference Between a Cat and a Comma?

Pronunciation point: As in the previous exercises, pausing and stress are important in speech. Plays on words often depend on contrast, and stress is used to bring out these contrasts.

This exercise also relates to syllable structure (onset versus rhyme), in that the onsets in Set 2 are transposed (in the same way as spoonerisms).

Minimum level: Intermediate

Exercise type: Learner production of passages (plays on words), individually or in pairs

Approximate time: 15 minutes

Preparation: Make one copy of the worksheet for each learner. Alternatively, to save paper, either make the worksheet accessible in soft copy on learners' devices, or show the worksheet on a screen.

Introducing the exercise: If you have not already completed the preceding exercises in this section, use the first play on words. In the question, *what's, difference, cat,* and *comma* will be stressed. In the answer, *cat, claws, end,* and *paws*; and *comma, pause, end*, and *clause*.

All the first set depend on homophones (words that are pronounced the same, but spelled differently).

The second set depend on spoonerisms; that is, changing the onsets (initial consonants, if any) of words.

Conducting the exercise: The structure of these examples may need a little explanation. The answers to the first example in each set are given.

♦ 75

Answers

Set 1

A prince is the heir to the throne. Water in a fountain is thrown to the air.

A man who has visited Niagara Falls has seen a mist. One who has not, has missed a scene.

A married man kisses his Mrs. A bachelor misses his kisses.

Set 2

A hostile audience boos madly. A sick cow moos badly.

A fisherman baits his hooks. A lazy schoolboy hates his books.

A cuddle is a bear hug. A louse is a hair bug.

A squeaking hinge begs to be oiled. The other is eggs to be boiled.

Sticky tape mends a tear. A stableboy tends a mare.

Worksheet

Set 1

Q: What's the difference between a cat and a comma?
A: A cat has claws at the end of its paws. A comma is a pause at the end of a clause.

Q: What's the difference between a prince and the water in a fountain?
A: A prince is the heir to the throne. Water in a fountain is . . . to the . . .

Q: What's the difference between a man who has visited Niagara Falls, and one who has not?
A: A man who has visited Niagara Falls has seen a mist. One who has not, has . . . a . . .

Q: What's the difference between a married man and a bachelor?
A: A married man kisses his Mrs. A bachelor . . . his . . .

Set 2

Q: What's the difference between a moldy lettuce and an unhappy song?
A: A moldy lettuce is a bad salad. An unhappy song is a sad ballad.

Q: What's the difference between a hostile audience and a sick cow?
A: A hostile audience boos madly. A sick cow . . .

Q: What's the difference between a fisherman and a lazy schoolboy?
A: A fisherman baits his hooks. A lazy schoolboy . . . his . . .

Q: What's the difference between a cuddle and a louse?
A: A cuddle is a bear hug. A louse is a . . .

Q: What's the difference between a squeaking hinge and eggs for breakfast?
A: A squeaking hinge begs to be oiled. The other is . . . to be. . .

Q: What's the difference between sticky tape and a stableboy?
A: Sticky tape mends a tear. A stableboy . . . a . . .

* This page is photocopiable for classroom use only.

B7

No, It Isn't

Pronunciation point: We saw in a previous exercise that, when a correction or contradiction is given, it is the part that is the correction/contradiction that carries the stress in a sentence:

When did you realize you liked math?
I DON'T like math.

Liking math has already been mentioned. It is the negative contained in *don't* that is the correction.

Minimum level: Elementary

Exercise type: A pairwork production exercise, with choice

Approximate time: 10 minutes (exercise), 5 minutes (debrief)

Preparation: Make one copy of Worksheet A for half the class, and of Worksheet B for the other half. For instance, in a class of 20, make ten copies of A and ten of B.

Introducing the exercise: Introduce the concept of correcting stress by, for example, asking a learner, "Is your name Maria Martinez?" to which she replies, "No. My name is Maria SUArez," with the stress on (the stressed syllable of) the correction.

Conducting the exercise: Divide the class into pairs. Give one member of each pair Worksheet A, and the other B. Explain that, when they start, A will choose either Question 1a or 1b, and ask it to B. B then responds with the correction shown in the picture, placing the stress on the correct part.

The teacher should wander around, listening to learners' responses and checking that they are stressing the right parts. For example, "Is it a photo of your hands?" should elicit "No. It's an X-ray of my hands" with the stress on X, while "Is it an X-ray of your foot?" should elicit "No. It's an X-ray of my HANDS" with the stress on *hands*.

Debrief: Reiterate that contrast is a strong factor in English pronunciation, and that the contrasted element is highlighted by stress, loudness, and intonation (especially a high fall).

Create your own materials: This is actually easy. Simply take a photo or other picture, e.g. a green apple. Then ask two questions relating to the different elements of the picture: "Is it a red apple?" or "Is it a green pear?"

Worksheet A

Ask your partner Questions 1, 3, 5, 7, 9. Choose either the a or b question.

When your partner asks you Questions 2, 4, 6, 8, 10, look at the picture, and respond with the sentence given, making sure you stress the correct part.

1a Is it a photo of your hands?
1b Is it an X-ray of your foot?

2   No. It's a dog's nose.

3a Is your picture two geese and six babies?
3b Is your picture two swans and three babies?

4   No. It's a waffle and strawberries.

5a Is your picture a helicopter flying?
5b Is your picture two jet planes flying?

6   No. It's the Hollywood sign.

7a Is your picture the dairy section in a supermarket?
7b Is your picture the checkout in a hardware store?

* This page is photocopiable for classroom use only.

8   No. A girl is feeding a pigeon.

9a Is your picture a schoolboy working on a smartphone?
9b Is your picture a businessman working on a laptop?

10 No. Mrs. Jones is my dentist.

* This page is photocopiable for classroom use only.

Worksheet B

Ask your partner Questions 2, 4, 6, 8, 10. Choose either the a or b question.

When your partner asks you Questions 1, 3, 5, 7, 9, look at the picture, and respond with the sentence given, making sure you stress the correct part.

1   No. It's an X-ray of my hands.

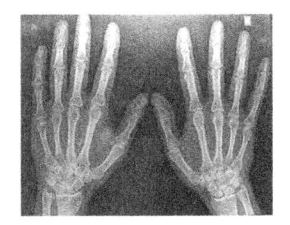

2a Is your picture a dog's tail?
2b Is your picture a cat's nose?

3   No. There are two swans and six babies.

4a Is your picture a waffle and blueberries?
4b Is your picture a pancake and strawberries?

5   No. It's two helicopters flying.

6a Does your picture show the Las Vegas sign?
6b Does your picture show a Hollywood street?

7   No. It's the checkout in a supermarket.

* This page is photocopiable for classroom use only.

8a   Is your picture a girl feeding a fish?
8b   Is your picture a boy feeding a pigeon?

9   No. It's a schoolboy working on a laptop.

10a Is Mr. Jones your dentist?
10b Is Mrs. Jones your doctor?

* This page is photocopiable for classroom use only.

B8
Let's Eat Grandpa

Pronunciation point: Pauses are a vital element in pronunciation.

Some pauses are necessary in speaking, if only to take breath. However, the placement of pauses is not random, but normally related to the grammar—that is, the meaning—of what is being said.

Minimum level: Elementary (depending on the passage). Passage 1 below is at elementary level, while 2 is at intermediate. Pauses have been inserted more liberally in the first passage, because of the level.

Exercise type: A paper exercise followed by pronunciation practice, for students working individually or in pairs

Approximate time: 15 minutes (exercise), 10 minutes (debrief)

Preparation: Make one copy of the worksheet for each learner. Alternatively, to save paper, either make the worksheet accessible in soft copy on learners' devices, or show the worksheet on a screen.

Introducing the exercise:

1. Elicit the meaning of *pause* from the students, and ask for suggestions as to why pauses are important in speech. You could use the title of this exercise. It has to be, "Let's eat, Grandpa!"; otherwise it sounds like cannibalism! There must be a comma (representing a pause) after *eat*, to show that you are addressing Grandpa.
2. The main functions of pauses are:
   - to show the listener (who can't see the script) what belongs together in terms of meaning and grammar, in the same way as punctuation in writing
   - to signal changes of topic (cf. paragraphs; see B3)
   - in dialogue, to show who is speaking
   - to emphasize that what you have just said is important

- to allow the speaker to take breath
- to prevent the speaker from speaking too fast

Conducting the exercise:

1. This exercise can be completed individually or in pairs or small groups.
2. Give one copy of the worksheet to each student. Point out that the passage looks strange because it has been printed without any punctuation.
3. Instruct the students to read through it until they understand it, and then put in the punctuation: commas, periods/full-stops (question marks, exclamation marks), and paragraph breaks, as well as quotation marks, capital letters, etc.
4. Once the punctuation has been agreed, ask the students to read the passage out loud, paying particular attention to pauses. A good rule of thumb is that a long pause will correspond to a paragraph break (that is, a change of topic or speaker); a medium pause to a sentence break (a period/full-stop, question mark, or exclamation mark, showing the end of a grammatically complete sentence); and a short pause to a comma or dash, showing that we are at the end of a stretch that belongs together but is not grammatically complete.

Create your own materials:

1. Choose a passage that is appropriate for the level of your learners. It could be a passage that they have already encountered in class. It could be one involving dialogue; that is, changes of speaker with long pauses (as in these passages).
2. Copy and paste a soft copy of the text, if available. Then, change everything to lower case letters (easily done on computer by highlighting the text and selecting "lower case"). Also, delete all punctuation, including paragraph breaks. Put back in the capital letters in names.
3. If a soft copy is not available, key in the text yourself, with no capital letters (except for names) or punctuation.

Passage 1: A Wet Day

Answer

There is no one right answer. However, here is one suggested answer.

a father and his young son/enjoyed going for long walks in the country // one day/as they were about to turn back/and go home/it suddenly began to pour with rain // they did not have an umbrella/or even raincoats with them/and there was nowhere to shelter from the rain/so they soon got very wet /// for a long time/as they were making the long walk back home/the boy was thinking // then/at last/he turned to his father/ and asked/why does it rain Dad // I don't like rain // it's unpleasant /// you may think it's unpleasant/but it's very useful/replied his father // you see/when it rains/water sinks into the ground/and then it helps the fruit and vegetables grow/for us to eat/and makes the grass grow long and green/for sheep and cows to eat /// as they walked on/the boy thought about this // finally/he said/if it rains to make the fruit vegetables and grass grow/then why does it rain on the road too

Here is the passage, with punctuation.

A father and his young son enjoyed going for long walks in the country. One day, as they were about to turn back and go home, it suddenly began to pour with rain. They did not have an umbrella or even raincoats with them, and there was nowhere to shelter from the rain, so they soon got very wet.

For a long time, as they were making the long walk back home, the boy was thinking. Then, at last, he turned to his father, and asked, "Why does it rain, Dad? I don't like rain. It's unpleasant."

"You may think it's unpleasant, but it's very useful," replied his father. "You see, when it rains, water sinks into the ground, and then it helps the fruit and vegetables grow for us to eat, and makes the grass grow long and green for sheep and cows to eat."

As they walked on, the boy thought about this. Finally, he said, "If it rains to make the fruit, vegetables, and grass grow, then why does it rain on the road too?"

Worksheet

The following passage has been printed here without any punctuation. However, it should be thought of as a script to be read aloud, as a teacher might to a class, or a parent to a child, rather than as a written passage to be punctuated. Where do you think the speaker should pause? Should it be a long, medium, or short pause? Put:

/ for a short pause
// for a medium pause
/// for a long pause

---

a father and his young son enjoyed going for long walks in the country one day as they were about to turn back and go home it suddenly began to pour with rain they did not have an umbrella or even raincoats with them and there was nowhere to shelter from the rain so they soon got very wet for a long time as they were making the long walk back home the boy was thinking then at last he turned to his father and asked why does it rain Dad I don't like rain it's unpleasant you may think it's unpleasant but it's very useful replied his father you see when it rains water sinks into the ground and then it helps the fruit and vegetables grow for us to eat and makes the grass grow long and green for sheep and cows to eat as they walked on the boy thought about this finally he said if it rains to make the fruit vegetables and grass grow then why does it rain on the road too

---

* This page is photocopiable for classroom use only.

Passage 2: A Fishing Trip Goes Wrong

Answer

There is no one right answer. However, here is one suggested answer.

one weekend/Robert/Bill/and Henry went on a fishing trip/in Henry's small boat // quite unexpectedly/a violent storm began/the giant waves tossing their small boat about/and smashing it into pieces // for three days/they floated on a small raft/with only some torn sheets/kitchen equipment/and an oil lamp // they had no food or drink/and the raft gave them no shelter from the burning sun/or the driving rain // finally/ in desperation/Bill/remembering the story of Aladdin/rubbed the lamp // a genie appeared/in a puff of smoke /// I will grant each of you one wish/he declared /// terrific/cried Henry // I want to go to the finest restaurant in our hometown /// the genie answered /your wish is granted/and Henry disappeared /// and I/added Robert/I want to go to my social club in our hometown /// your wish is granted too/said the genie/and Robert disappeared as well /// and you/Bill/what is your wish/the genie asked the last survivor /// er/I feel lonely now/answered Bill sadly // I wish Robert and Henry were here

Here is the original passage, with punctuation.

One weekend, Robert, Bill, and Henry went on a fishing trip in Henry's small boat. Quite unexpectedly, a violent storm began, the giant waves tossing their small boat about and smashing it into pieces. For three days, they floated on a small raft with only some torn sheets, kitchen equipment, and an oil lamp. They had no food or drink, and the raft gave them no shelter from the burning sun or the driving rain. Finally in desperation, Bill, remembering the story of Aladdin, rubbed the lamp. A genie appeared in a puff of smoke.

"I will grant each of you one wish," he declared.

"Terrific!" cried Henry. "I want to go to the finest restaurant in our hometown."

The genie answered, "Your wish is granted." And Henry disappeared.

"And I," added Robert, "I want to go to my social club in our hometown."

"Your wish is granted too," said the genie, and Robert disappeared as well.

"And you, Bill, what is your wish?" the genie asked the last survivor.

"Er . . . I feel lonely now," answered Bill sadly. "I wish Robert and Henry were here."

Worksheet

The following passage has been printed here without any punctuation. However, it should be thought of as a script to be read aloud, as a teacher might to a class, or a parent to a child, rather than as a written passage to be punctuated. Where do you think the speaker should pause? Should it be a long, medium, or short pause? Put:

/ for a short pause
// for a medium pause
/// for a long pause

---

one weekend Robert Bill and Henry went on a fishing trip in Henry's small boat quite unexpectedly a violent storm began the giant waves tossing their small boat about and smashing it into pieces for three days they floated on a small raft with only some torn sheets kitchen equipment and an oil lamp they had no food or drink and the raft gave them no shelter from the burning sun or the driving rain finally in desperation Bill remembering the story of Aladdin rubbed the lamp a genie appeared in a puff of smoke I will grant each of you one wish he declared terrific cried Henry I want to go to the finest restaurant in our hometown the genie answered your wish is granted and Henry disappeared and I added Robert I want to go to my social club in our hometown your wish is granted too said the genie and Robert disappeared as well and you Bill what is your wish the genie asked the last survivor er I feel lonely now answered Bill sadly I wish Robert and Henry were here

---

* This page is photocopiable for classroom use only.

Section C
Word Stress

C1
BRAzil, braZIL?

Pronunciation point: The correct placement of stress in multisyllable words is important for recognition of the word, and must therefore be learned when the word is learned. There is thus a large difference in pronunciation and perception between *insight* (*INsight*) and *incite* (*inCITE*) (where the capital letters indicate the stressed syllable).

Minimum level: Two exercises are supplied here, both at elementary level.

Exercise type: A worksheet exercise, individually or in pairs. It can be made into a race, seeing who finishes first.

Approximate time: 5 minutes (pre-teaching), 15 minutes (exercise), 5 minutes (debrief)

Preparation: Make one copy of the worksheet for each learner. Alternatively, to save paper, either make the worksheet accessible in soft copy on learners' devices, or show the worksheet on a screen.

Introducing the exercise: Illustrate the stress placement in multisyllable words by using words like *register* (stress on the first syllable, thus *REgister*, not *reGISter* or *regisTER*), *computer* (stress on the second syllable, thus *comPUter*), and *absentee* (stress on the third syllable, thus *absenTEE*). Non-verbal features can reinforce this, e.g. beats with the hands, facial expressions such as nodding or raising the eyebrows on the stressed syllables.

Conducting the exercise: Distribute the worksheet (or show it on screen) and instruct learners to move from the bottom of the diagram to the top, only going through places with second syllable stress ("Susan") and stress later than the second syllable ("David"). You could perhaps start them off by asking which is the first place they go through (*Brazil* for Susan; *Argentina* for David).

Answers:

("Susan") Brazil—Jamaica—Peru—Japan—Nepal—Kuwait—Malaysia—Bahamas—Morocco

("David") *Argentina—Ethiopia—Mozambique—Indonesia—Madagascar—Bangladesh—Venezuela—Senegal—Vietnam*

Debriefing note: You could ask learners to say which syllable the stress is on in all the place names.

These are the stressed syllables in the English pronunciation of the names of these countries. This may differ from the way nationals of the countries pronounce them, because of differences in the way stress is used in their languages, etc. It may also be different from the way the words are pronounced as names, e.g. the British linguist David Brazil, referred to in B3, was DAvid BRAzil.

Create your own materials:

- Use a maze format.
- Decide on the pronunciation feature to be used.
- List some words that (i) are, and (ii) are not examples of that feature.
- Plot the correct path through the maze, and write the exemplar words in those places. Then fill in the other places with the distractors.

Worksheet

Where is Susan?

Susan loves traveling. However, she only wants to go to countries that have stress on the second syllable (of the English pronunciation of the country's name). Starting at the bottom of the page, and only traveling (forwards, backwards, or sideways) to countries that have stress on the second syllable, where does she travel?

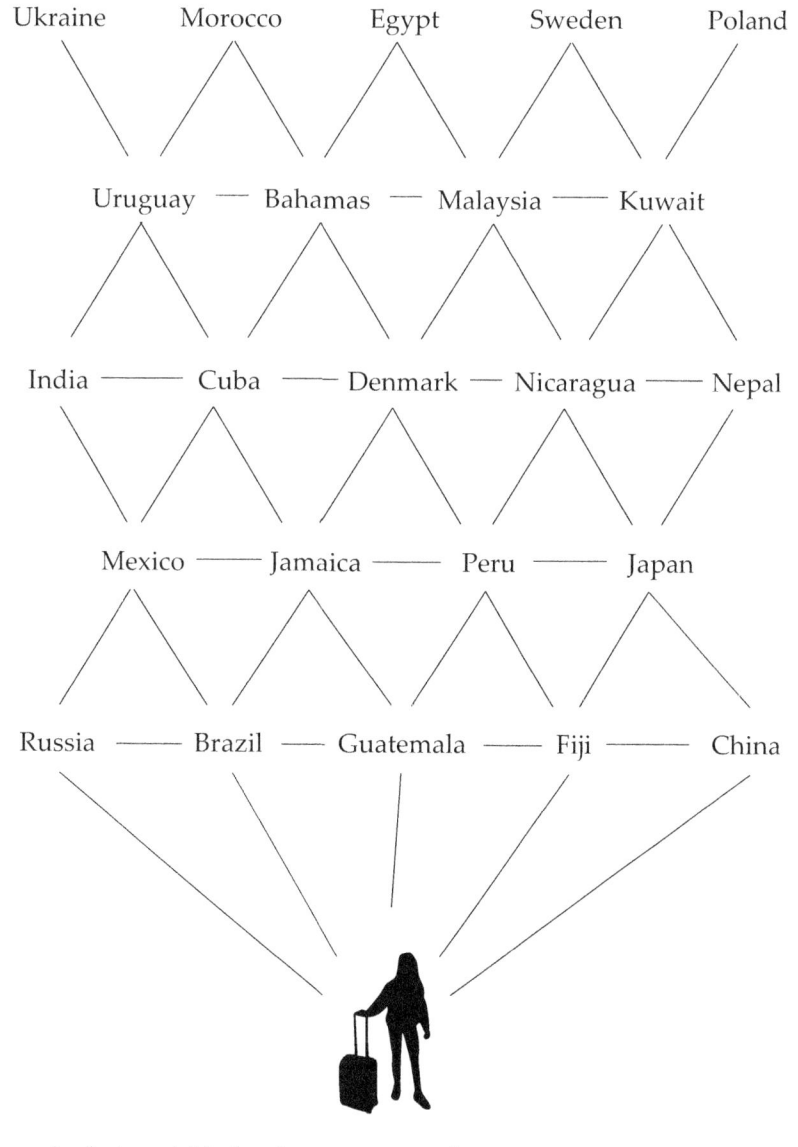

Ukraine   Morocco   Egypt   Sweden   Poland

Uruguay — Bahamas — Malaysia — Kuwait

India — Cuba — Denmark — Nicaragua — Nepal

Mexico — Jamaica — Peru — Japan

Russia — Brazil — Guatemala — Fiji — China

* This page is photocopiable for classroom use only.

Worksheet

Where is David?

David loves traveling. However, he only wants to go to countries that do not have stress on the first or second syllable (of the English pronunciation of the country's name). That is, the primary stress is on the third or later syllable. Starting at the bottom of the page, and only traveling (forwards, backwards, or sideways) to countries that have stress on the third or later syllable, where does he travel?

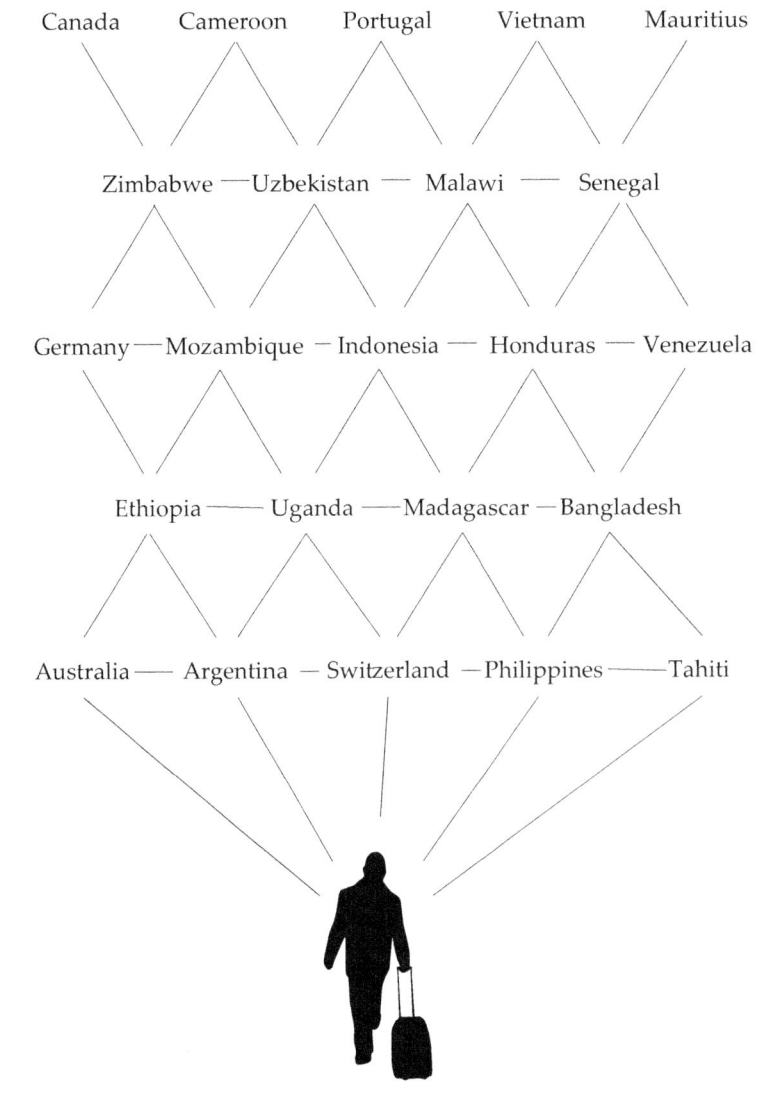

Canada   Cameroon   Portugal   Vietnam   Mauritius

Zimbabwe — Uzbekistan — Malawi — Senegal

Germany — Mozambique — Indonesia — Honduras — Venezuela

Ethiopia — Uganda — Madagascar — Bangladesh

Australia — Argentina — Switzerland — Philippines — Tahiti

* This page is photocopiable for classroom use only.

C2

EDucation, eDUcation, educAtion, educaTION?

Pronunciation point: It is important that speakers place the stress on the right syllable in words that have many syllables because that is one of the major cues that allow listeners to recognize the word being spoken.

Minimum level: Intermediate

Exercise type: A maze, to be completed individually

Approximate time: 15 minutes (exercise), 10 minutes (debrief)

Preparation: Make one copy of the worksheet for each learner. Alternatively, to save paper, either make the worksheet accessible in soft copy on learners' devices, or show the worksheet on a screen.

Introducing the exercise: Use a word that the learners are familiar with. It could be a place name: *Alabama* or *Nottinghamshire*. Pronounce it in four different ways: with the stress on the first, second, third, and fourth syllables (*Alabama, aLAbama, alaBAma, alabaMA*). Ask the learners which one sounds right.

Conducting the exercise: Distribute the worksheet. All the words have four syllables. Learners start at the bottom left (*education*). If the stress is on the first syllable, they go south (downwards); on the second, north (upwards); on the third, east (to the right); and on the fourth, west (to the left).

Debrief notes: The correct sequence is *education* (3rd), *Filipino* (3rd), *psychology* (2nd), *curriculum* (2nd), *bachelorette* (4th), *majority* (2nd), *Senegalese* (4th), *Elizabeth* (2nd), *experiment* (2nd), *population* (3rd), *entertainment* (3rd), *emergency* (2nd), *American* (2nd), *conversation* (3rd), *disadvantage* (3rd), *television* (1st), *polytechnic* (3rd), *information* (3rd), *calculator* (1st), *agriculture* (1st), *interviewee* (4th), *biodegrade* (4th), *ceremony* (1st), *alligator* (1st), *satisfaction* (3rd), *Bangladeshi* (3rd), *architecture* (1st), *Alexander* (3rd), *championship* (1st), *bureaucratic* (3rd). The exit gate is thus #16.

Create your own materials: Websites contain lists of words with one, two, three, four, etc. syllables. A maze-type puzzle can be easily created. At lower levels, shorter words can be used.

Worksheet

All the words in the grid below contain four syllables. However, they may be stressed on the first, second, third, or fourth syllable. Start at the bottom left with the word *education*.

If the word is stressed:

- on the first syllable, move southwards ⇨
- on the second syllable, move northwards ⇧
- on the third syllable, move eastwards ⇦
- on the fourth syllable, move westwards ⇩

At which gate (1–16) do you exit the grid?

1	2	3	4	5	6	7	8	
integrity	generator	conversation	disadvantage	television	democratic	relationship	ecosystem	9
watermelon	historical	American	intelligence	polytechnic	information	calculator	Argentina	10
population	entertainment	emergency	disappointment	responsible	Penelope	agriculture	accessories	11
experiment	avocado	anatomy	environment	ceremony	biodegrade	interviewee	biology	12
Elizabeth	Senegalese	inspiration	photography	alligator	consequences	Cinderella	complicated	13
developer	majority	bachelorette	mechanism	satisfaction	Bangladeshi	architecture	automatic	14
preposition	discovery	curriculum	helicopter	authority	republican	Alexander	championship	15
education	Filipino	psychology	macaroni	independence	caterpillar	apostrophe	bureaucratic	16

⇧

* This page is photocopiable for classroom use only.

EDucation, eDUcation, eduCAtion, educaTION?

C3

She Was Presented With a Present

Pronunciation point: As we have seen, multisyllable words have strong stress on one syllable and, vice versa, do not have strong stress on the other syllables, in order for it to be clear which syllable is the stressed one. The correct placement of stress is important for listeners to recognize the word being pronounced.

There is a group of two-syllable words which may have stress on the first syllable if they are being used grammatically as nouns (or occasionally adjectives), but on the second syllable if they are verbs.

Minimum level: Intermediate

Exercise type: In fact, a grammatical recognition exercise, to be completed individually or in pairs. The pronunciation factor comes in the debrief.

Approximate time: 10 minutes (exercise), 15 minutes (debrief)

Preparation: Make one copy of the worksheet for each learner. Alternatively, to save paper, either make the worksheet accessible in soft copy on learners' devices, or show the worksheet on a screen.

Introducing the exercise: Use the common word *present*, as in the title of this exercise. Illustrate that, when it is a noun, as in *birthday present*, the stress is on the first syllable (*PREsent*). Similarly, if it is an adjective, as in *the present day*, it is also on the first syllable. However, if it is a verb, as in *to present awards*, the stress is on the second syllable (*preSENT*). Note that the segments (especially the vowels) may change, and that the stressed syllable is shown in transcription by a superscript ' : /ˈprezənt, prɪˈzent/.

Conducting the exercise: Recap the definition of nouns and verbs with the class. Many of the examples in this exercise involve inflected forms of the nouns or verbs (see the *Debrief notes* at the end of this exercise). They may include adjectives that are inflected forms of verbs, e.g. *updated*.

The learners decide whether the underlined words in the sentences are nouns or verbs, and they circle the letter in the correct column. For example, in *Last year was the warmest winter on record*, *record* is a noun, so the letter S should be circled.

If they circle the correct letters, they form the sentence, "Stress the right syllable."

This is a grammatical exercise and should be fairly easy for learners who understand grammatical categories. The real purpose of the exercise, however, is the difference in stress placement, which should be covered at some length in the debrief.

Debrief notes: This exercise is in fact a grammatical exercise. From the grammatical point of view, nouns can be identified by

- having -*s* that makes them plural, e.g. *insults*
- having -*'s* or -*s'* for the singular or plural possessive, e.g. *desert's, rebels'*
- coming before, and modifying another noun, e.g. *permit holder*
- coming after an article, e.g. *an extract*
- coming after a preposition, e.g. *on the subject*

Verbs can be identified by:

- having -*(e)d* that makes them
  - the past tense, e.g. *contracted* (#9)
  - a verb participle, e.g. *projected* (#14)
  - a verb participle functioning as an adjective, e.g. *updated* (#6), clearly from the verb *update*
  - a verb participle functioning as an adjective, e.g. *concerted* (#20), not so clearly from the formal, somewhat archaic verb *concert*
- having -*ing*, e.g. *progressing*
- coming after "infinitive *to*," e.g. *to convert*
- coming after a noun or pronoun that is its subject, e.g. *you digest*

The important point is that, during the debrief, the teacher illustrates, and gets the learners to pronounce, the stress patterns of the various words and uses, clearly distinguishing first- and second-syllable stress.

Create your own materials: Here are (admittedly less common) words that behave the same way: *abstract, compound, compress, conflict, consort, contest, contrast, convict, decrease, defect, detail, discharge, discount, escort, export, frequent, implant, import, increase, insert, invite, misprint, perfect, perfume, present, proceeds, produce, protest, refund, refuse, retard, rewrite, segment, survey, torment, transfer*. Note that sometimes the meaning is somewhat different, e.g. *They refused to cooperate* versus *There was refuse on the streets*.

Also, not all pairs of noun/verb pairs behave this way. There is a word formation process known as conversion, whereby words that are one grammatical category (e.g. *carpet*, a noun as in *We fitted new carpet*) comes to be used in a different grammatical category (e.g. a verb, as in *We carpeted the living room*). Both have first-syllable stress: *CARpet*.

Worksheet

Nouns are naming words for things, people, animals, places, characteristics, and ideas. Verbs are doing words describing actions, states, or occurrences.

Decide if the underlined words in these sentences are nouns or verbs—as they are used in the sentences. If they are nouns, circle the letter in the noun column, or in the verb column for a verb. Then the letters go together to form a sentence.

#	Sentence	Noun	Verb
1	Last year was the warmest winter on <u>record</u>.	S	T
2	This month's sales are a 3% <u>increase</u> on last month's.	T	H
3	I need to <u>convert</u> this file from html to Word.	E	R
4	He wrote a series of books on the <u>subject</u> of Buddhism.	E	U
5	Make sure you <u>digest</u> your lunch before playing football.	P	S
6	He installed the <u>updated</u> version of the software.	I	S
7	The <u>rebels'</u> leader tried to take the president prisoner.	T	B
8	The university <u>rejects</u> a third of all applicants.	O	H
9	The child <u>contracted</u> the flu from his mother.	D	E
10	Car parking for <u>permit</u> holders only.	R	W
11	The building of the house is <u>progressing</u> according to schedule.	N	I
12	The teams were shouting <u>insults</u> at each other.	G	C
13	She read an <u>extract</u> from her latest book.	H	R
14	As the population ages, the cost of health care is <u>projected</u> to rise.	F	T
15	The goods were <u>transported</u> by sea.	M	S
16	Middlesbrough beating Manchester City was a major <u>upset</u>.	Y	C
17	It was a steep <u>incline</u>, and they soon started sweating.	L	A
18	The police <u>suspected</u> that he was lying.	K	L
19	The region will become drier and the <u>desert's</u> size will increase.	A	E
20	All countries need to make a <u>concerted</u> effort to fight global warming.	V	B
21	Local residents <u>objected</u> to the proposed road.	I	L
22	She judged him by his <u>conduct</u>.	E	Y

* This page is photocopiable for classroom use only.

C4

Edinburgh, eDINburgh, edinBURGH?

Pronunciation point: The correct placement of stress in multisyllable words is important for recognition of the word, and must therefore be learned when the word is learned.

This exercise uses British place names, although they are stressed the same in both BrE and AmE.

Minimum level: Elementary

Exercise type: An individual worksheet exercise. It can be made into a race, seeing who finishes first.

Approximate time: 10 minutes (exercise), 5 minutes (debrief)

Preparation: Make one copy of the worksheet for each learner. Alternatively, to save paper, either make the worksheet accessible in soft copy on learners' devices, or show the worksheet on a screen.

Introducing the exercise: Do the first road sign, as an example. *nortHAMPton* has second-syllable stress, while *AberDEEN* has third-syllable.

Conducting the exercise: Distribute the worksheets (or show it on screen) and instruct learners to identify places that have third-syllable stress, and then follow the arrows and roads.

Answers: The correct route is *AberDEEN, InverNESS, Bognor REgis, WolverHAMPton, Milton KEYNES, Stoke-on-TRENT, John o' GROATS*.

Here are all the 25 places, with their stress patterns.

1st syllable	2nd syllable	3rd syllable
Cambridge	Armagh	Aberdeen
Cardiff	Northampton	Bognor Regis
Edinburgh	Northumberland	Inverness
Gloucester	Southampton	John o' Groats
Hereford	St Albans	Milton Keynes
Lincoln	St Leonards	Stoke-on-Trent
Liverpool	West Bromwich	Wolverhampton
Norwich		
Peterborough		
Salisbury		
Sunderland		

Worksheet

Drive from the bottom of the page to the top, only going through places that have stress on the third syllable.

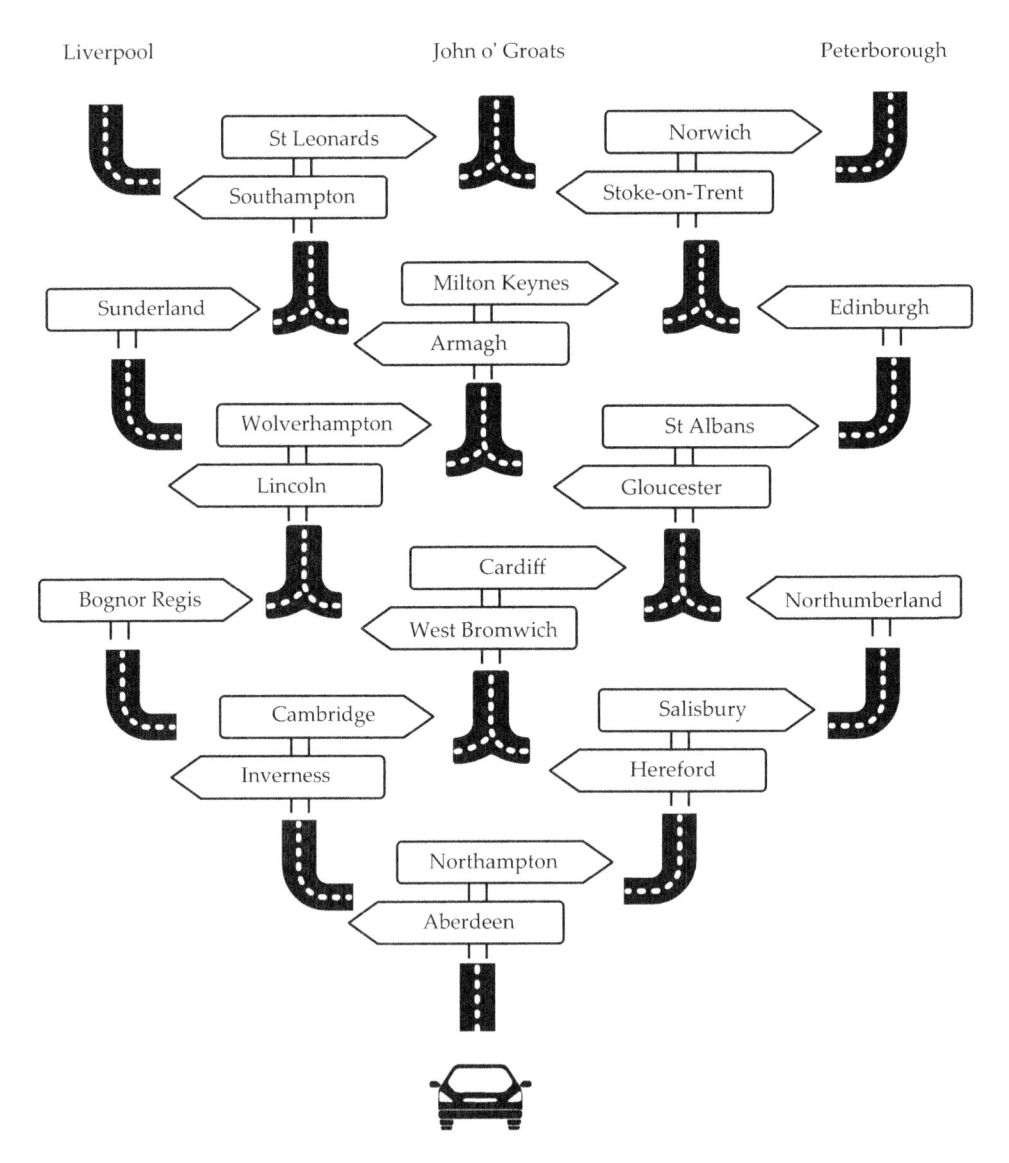

Liverpool　　　　　　　John o' Groats　　　　　　Peterborough

- St Leonards
- Southampton
- Sunderland
- Milton Keynes
- Armagh
- Norwich
- Stoke-on-Trent
- Edinburgh
- Wolverhampton
- Lincoln
- St Albans
- Gloucester
- Bognor Regis
- Cardiff
- West Bromwich
- Northumberland
- Cambridge
- Inverness
- Salisbury
- Hereford
- Northampton
- Aberdeen

* This page is photocopiable for classroom use only.

C5

Letter from London

Pronunciation point: The correct placement of stress in multisyllable words is important for recognition of the word, and must therefore be learned when the word is learned.

This exercise uses U.S. state names, although they are stressed the same in both AmE and BrE.

Minimum level: Elementary

Exercise type: An individual worksheet exercise. It can be made into a race, seeing who finishes first.

Approximate time: 10 minutes (exercise), 5 minutes (debrief)

Preparation: Make one copy of the worksheet for each learner. Alternatively, to save paper, either make the worksheet accessible in soft copy on learners' devices, or show the worksheet on a screen.

Introducing the exercise: Do the first three states, as an example. *Alabama* (3rd syllable), *Alaska* (2nd), *Arkansas* (1st). Pronounce them all possible ways: *Alabama, aLAbama, alaBAma, alabaMA*. It is usually very clear to the learners which one is correct.

Conducting the exercise: Distribute the worksheets (or show it on screen). Tell the learners they are on holiday in London, and instruct them to post their letters in the postboxes by writing the names of the states under the postbox with the right stress pattern.

Answers: Here are all the 40 one-word states of the USA, with their stress patterns.

1st syllable	2nd syllable	3rd or later syllable
Arkansas	Alaska	Alabama
Delaware	Connecticut	Arizona
Florida	Hawaii	California
Georgia	Kentucky	Colorado
Idaho	Missouri	Illinois
Iowa	Montana	Indiana
Kansas	Nebraska	Louisiana (4th)
Maine	Nevada	Massachusetts
Maryland	Ohio	Minnesota
Michigan	Vermont	Mississippi
Oregon	Virginia	Oklahoma
Texas	Wisconsin	Pennsylvania
Utah	Wyoming	Tennessee
Washington		

You might want to cover all 40 of them.

Worksheet

Sort the following letters according to the stress pattern (on the 1st, 2nd, or 3rd syllable) of the name of the state. Write the name of the state under the correct mailbox.

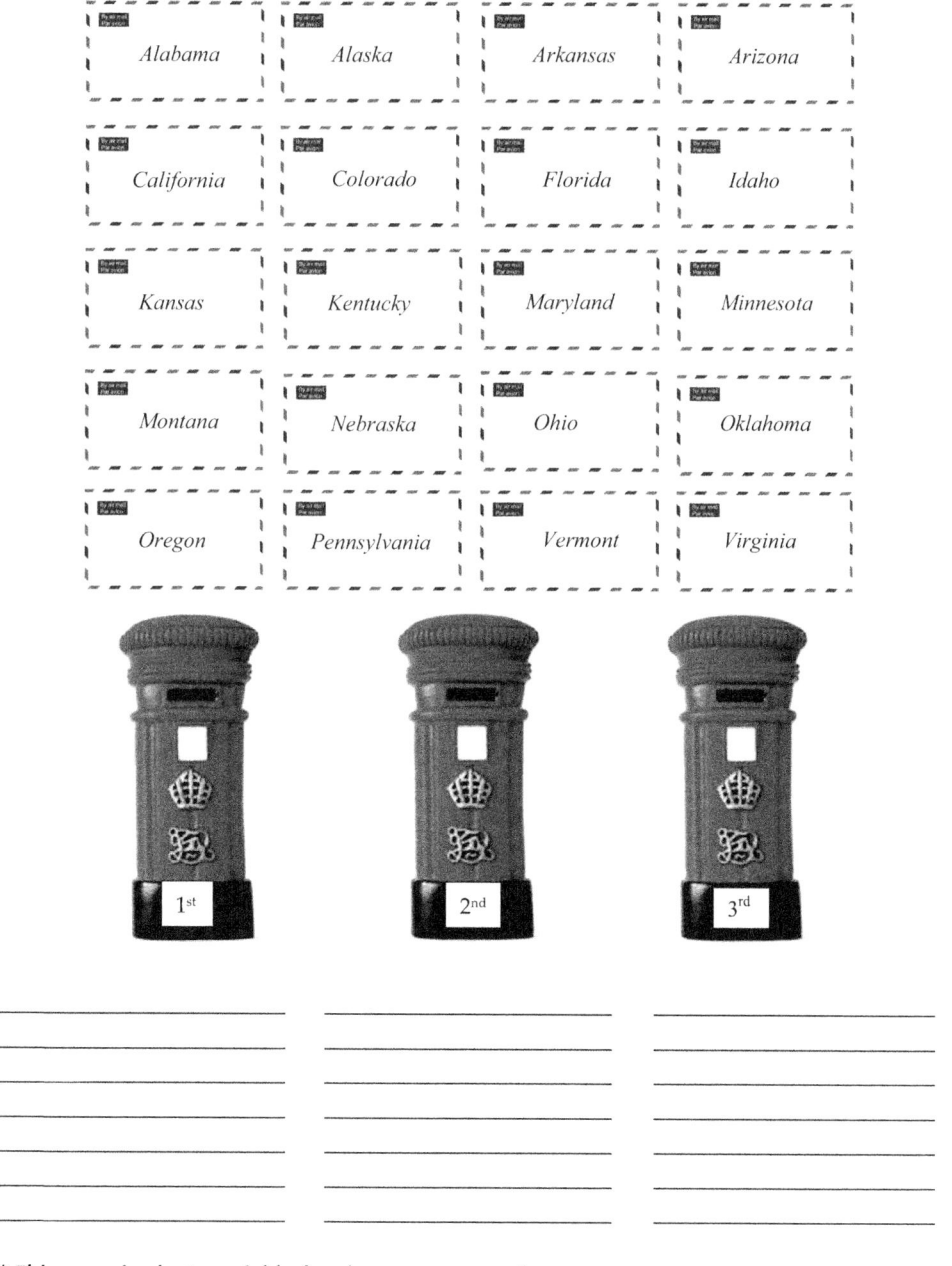

Alabama	Alaska	Arkansas	Arizona
California	Colorado	Florida	Idaho
Kansas	Kentucky	Maryland	Minnesota
Montana	Nebraska	Ohio	Oklahoma
Oregon	Pennsylvania	Vermont	Virginia

1st   2nd   3rd

* This page is photocopiable for classroom use only.

Section D
Spelling and Phonemic Symbols

D1

Eh, Bee, Sea, . . .

Pronunciation point: There is a difference—and sometimes a large difference—between the names that are given to letters of the Roman alphabet used for English, and the sounds that those letters typically represent. Confusion between the two may lead to misspellings and mispronunciations.

Minimum level: Elementary

Exercise type: An individual sorting game

Approximate time: 10 minutes (exercise), 10 minutes (debrief)

Preparation: Make one copy of the worksheet for each learner. Alternatively, to save paper, either make the worksheet accessible in soft copy on learners' devices, or show the worksheet on a screen.

Introducing the exercise: Ask the learners how letters of the alphabet are named in their native language. (This requires an alphabetic system, so cannot be used for Chinese, Japanese, etc.). Point out that in English, the name of the letter may not be a reliable indication of the sound the letter usually makes. With younger learners, you could teach them the "Alphabet Song" ("Now I know my ABC"); many versions are available online, on YouTube, etc.

Conducting the exercise: The learners say the names of the letters out loud. They sort them into boxes according to the vowel sound the name contains.

Debrief notes: The answers are:

/iː/	/e/	/eɪ/	/uː/	Others
B /biː/	F /ef/	A /eɪ/	Q /kjuː/	I /aɪ/
C /siː/	L /el/	H /eɪtʃ/	U /juː/	O /əʊ ~ oʊ/
D /diː/	M /em/	J /dʒeɪ/	W /dʌbəl juː/	R /ɑː(r)/
E /iː/	N /en/	K /keɪ/		Y /waɪ/
G /dʒiː/	S /es/			
P /piː/	X /eks/			
T /tiː/	Z /zed/ (BrE)			
V /viː/				
Z /ziː/ (AmE)				

Points to make:

- The name of the letter and the sound that it typically makes are different things.
- The name of the letter and the sound that it typically makes are not usually the same.
- The name of a letter may not be the most common sound that it represents, e.g. G is not usually /dʒ/.
- The name of a letter may not even contain the sound that it typically makes, e.g. H, Q, R (for BrE), W, Y.
- The names of the letters of the Roman alphabet in English may differ from their names in other languages (French, etc.).

Worksheet

The letters of the Roman alphabet used for English (A, B, C, etc.) have names. However, these names may not be a reliable indication of the sounds the letters represent.

Take the 26 letters of the alphabet: A, B, C, D, E, F, G, H, I, J, K, L, M, N, O, P, Q, R, S, T, U, V, W, X, Y, Z. Sort them into the correct mailbox according to the vowel sound their names contain. A and B are done for you.

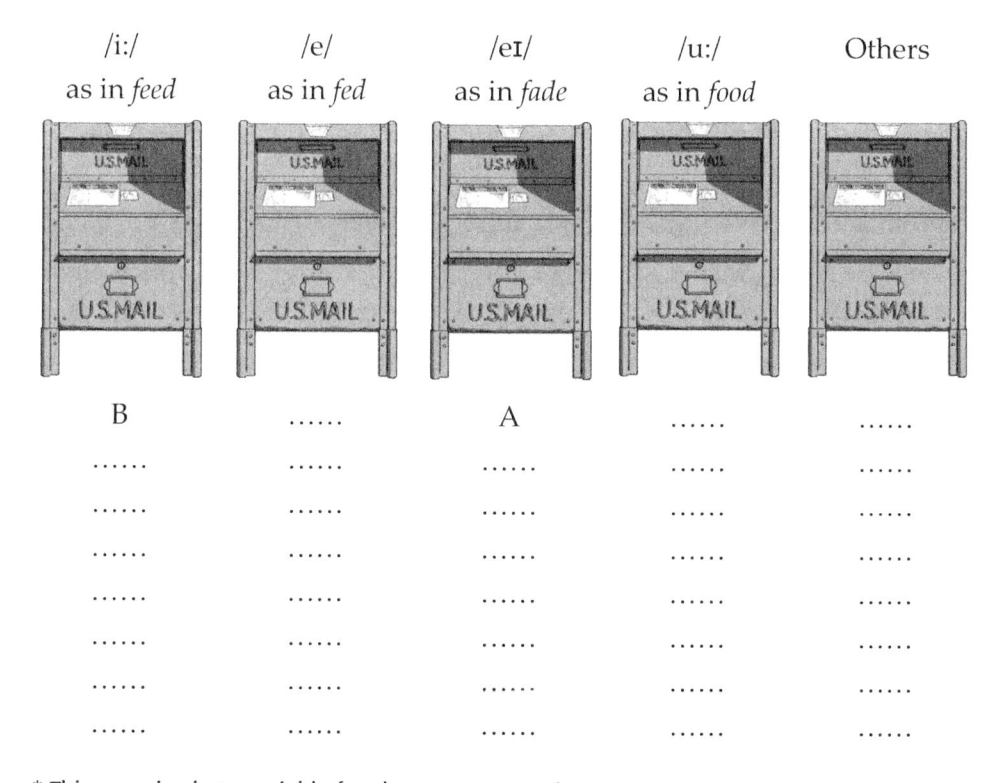

/iː/ as in *feed*	/e/ as in *fed*	/eɪ/ as in *fade*	/uː/ as in *food*	Others
B	……	A	……	……
……	……	……	……	……
……	……	……	……	……
……	……	……	……	……
……	……	……	……	……
……	……	……	……	……
……	……	……	……	……
……	……	……	……	……

* This page is photocopiable for classroom use only.

D2

We Joined the Navy to See the World

Pronunciation point: English has many homophones; that is, words that are pronounced the same but spelled differently. This shows that the spelling system of English is not very regular. Homophones do not occur, or are much less common, in other languages.

Minimum level: Elementary (depending on vocabulary level)

Exercise type: A mistake-spotting exercise, to be completed individually or in pairs

Approximate time: 10 minutes (exercise), 20 minutes (debrief)

Preparation: Make one copy of the worksheet for each learner. Alternatively, to save paper, either make the worksheet accessible in soft copy on learners' devices, or show the worksheet on a screen.

Introducing the exercise: Explain the concept of homophones. The somewhat cryptic title of this exercise comes from the 1936 Fred Astaire and Ginger Rogers film *Follow the Fleet*, and goes: "We joined the navy to see the world. And what did we see? We saw the sea." That is, the English words *see* and *sea* are homophones.

Conducting the exercise: The passage contains a number of homophones; that is, words that are pronounced the same as, but spelled differently from, the intended words. Learners identify the misspellings and correct them. Encourage the use of dictionaries (printed or online) for any words the learners are not sure of.

Debrief notes: Here are the misspelled (homophone) words with the intended words/spellings.

son: sun	*maze: maize*	*bored: board*
see: sea	*dear: deer*	*suites: sweets*
mourning: morning	*meet: meat*	*stake: steak*
serials: cereals	*sighed: side*	*pi: pie*
pairs: pears	*hair: hare*	*byte: bite*
plumbs: plums	*whine**: wine*	*place: plaice*
buries: berries	*would: wood*	*friar: fryer (frier)*****
currents: currants	*heir: air*	*been: bean*
bred: bread	*roles: rolls*	*tee: tea*
muscles: mussels	*leak: leek*	*due: dew*
chutes: shoots	*carat: carrot*	*route*****: root*
time: thyme	*tale: tail*	*sheikhs: shakes*
chilly: chilli*	*desert***: dessert*	*biers: beers*
hole: whole	*moose: mousse*	*licker: liquor*
flower: flour	*doe: dough* (or *donuts*)	

* There are other possible spellings.
** A few accents distinguish these two.
*** Meaning "abandon."
**** *Frier* is much less common alternative.
***** Provided it is pronounced to rhyme with *boot*.

You could go through the phonemic transcriptions of these words with the learners. Since the words are homophones, there is only one transcription for each pair.

Create your own materials: A comprehensive list of homophones in (British) English is given by Higgins (2018). Look through them, and think up a scenario in which several of them may appear, e.g. food in a menu. Create a passage or other document using the wrong spelling of the intended homophone. Some ingenuity is required.

Worksheet

Here is a hotel menu. Correct any words that are misspelled.

Son and See Hotel
Menu

Breakfast (Available Until 11 in the Mourning)
Choice of serials
Choice of fruits: pairs, plumbs, buries, currents, etc.
Choice of bred and jams

Lunch/Dinner
Thai red curry with muscles, cooked with bamboo chutes, time, and chilly
Hole prawns, tossed in flower and fried, with mushrooms and maze
Venison (dear) meet loaf, with a sighed salad
Jugged hair, cooked in red whine
Would-fired pizza
Heir-fried egg roles

Soups
Leak soup
Carat soup
Ox tale soup

Desert
Chocolate moose
Doe nuts
Cheese bored
See the display cabinet for more suites

Children's Menu
Stake and kidney pi
Byte-sized chicken nuggets
Place and chips, cooked in the air friar
Cheese omelet with baked been salad

Drinks
Tee or coffee
Soft drinks (Coke, Pepsi, Mountain Due, route beer, Dr. Brown's, etc.)
Milk sheikhs
Wines, biers
We do not serve hard licker

* This page is photocopiable for classroom use only.

D3

Around the World in 20 Countries

Pronunciation point: The ability to recognize words given in phonemic transcription is necessary in order to be able to use a dictionary to check pronunciation. This exercise uses British English pronunciation.

Minimum level: Elementary

Exercise type: An individual wordsearch, but using phonemic symbols rather than spelling

Approximate time: 15 minutes (exercise), 10 minutes (debrief)

Preparation: Make one copy of the worksheet for each learner. Alternatively, to save paper, either make the worksheet accessible in soft copy on learners' devices, or show the worksheet on a screen.

Introducing the exercise: Ask students whether they are familiar with the wordsearch format. Explain that this one uses the same rules (words can be written in any direction) but with phonemic symbols rather than spelling. In any case, one word (*Singapore*) has been highlighted to make things clear.

Conducting the exercise: Distribute the worksheet (or show it on screen), and tell students to find the names of 20 countries (including *Singapore*) in the wordsearch. If you feel that, by giving them the capital cities, they would not search the square so carefully, hide the capital cities until they have had a few minutes to search. However, this is a pronunciation/transcription exercise, not a geography exercise, so hints such as the capital cities should be given sometime.

Answers

Beijing	China	tʃaɪnə
Berne	Switzerland	swɪtsələnd
Cairo	Egypt	iːdʒɪpt
Cardiff	Wales	weɪlz
Havana	Cuba	kjuːbə
Kampala	Uganda	juːgændə
Lima	Peru	pəruː
London	England	ɪŋglənd
Madrid	Spain	speɪn
Manila	Philippines	fɪlɪpiːnz
Mexico City	Mexico	meksɪkəʊ
Moscow	Russia	rʌʃə
Ottawa	Canada	kænədə
Panama City	Panama	pænəmɑː
Reykjavik	Iceland	aɪslənd
Suva	Fiji	fiːdʒiː
Taipei	Taiwan	taɪwɑːn
Tehran	Iran	ɪrɑːn
Vientiane	Laos	laʊs

Create your own: There are several websites that allow you to create your own wordsearches. However, they work with words in regular English spelling. In order to create a wordsearch in phonemic transcription:

- Decide what your words will be.
- Make sure you know how to transcribe them correctly.
- Devise a system for entering phonemic symbols that are not Roman alphabet letters. For example, the Roman alphabet letters *c, q, x,* and *y* are not used for English phonemic transcription, so they can be substituted for phonemic symbols such as ʃ, ŋ, ə and ɔ.
- Use an online website to generate the wordsearch, for instance Discovery Education (n.d.).

You may still be able to add a word or two to the generated wordsearch, and generally tidy it up.

Worksheet

Find the names of 20 countries in this wordsearch. The names have been written in phonemic symbols. They may be horizontal, vertical or diagonal in any direction. To start you off, *Singapore* has been highlighted in the first row. If you are really stuck, the capital cities of the countries are given underneath the puzzle as a clue.

æ	s	ɪ	ŋ	ə	p	ɔː	dʒ	aɪ	l
f	w	ŋ	ɪ	ʃ	æ	m	s	t	m
iː	ɪ	g	j	ʌ	n	l	aʊ	s	e
dʒ	t	l	ɜː	r	ə	b	uː	j	k
iː	s	ə	ɪ	n	m	ɪ	f	ɔː	s
dʒ	ə	n	d	p	ɑː	r	w	p	ɪ
ɪ	l	d	tʃ	ə	iː	ɑː	eɪ	ə	k
p	ə	aɪ	s	ʌ	n	n	l	r	əʊ
t	n	ɑː	w	aɪ	t	æ	z	uː	p
ə	d	n	æ	g	uː	j	k	ɔɪ	r

Capital Cities

Beijing	Berne	Cairo	Cardiff	Havana
Kampala	Lima	London	Madrid	Manila
Mexico City	Moscow	Ottawa	Panama City	Reykjavik
Suva	Taipei	Tehran	Vientiane	

* This page is photocopiable for classroom use only.

D4

D'you Know the Capital of Alaska?

Pronunciation point: The ability to recognize words given in phonemic transcription is necessary in order to be able to use a dictionary to check pronunciation. This exercise uses American English pronunciation.

Minimum level: Elementary

Exercise type: An individual wordsearch, but using phonemic symbols rather than spelling

Approximate time: 15 minutes (exercise), 10 minutes (debrief)

Preparation: Make one copy of the worksheet for each learner. Alternatively, to save paper, either make the worksheet accessible in soft copy on learners' devices, or show the worksheet on a screen.

Introducing the exercise: Ask students whether they are familiar with the wordsearch format. Explain that this one uses the same rules (words can be written in any direction) but with phonemic symbols rather than spelling. In any case, one word (*Juneau*) has been highlighted to make things clear.

Conducting the exercise: Distribute the worksheet (or show it on screen), and tell students to find the names of 20 US state capitals (including *Juneau*) in the wordsearch. The title of this exercise is a well-known joke in the USA, *d'you know* being pronounced the same as *Juneau*. If you feel that, by giving them the states, they would not search the square so carefully, hide the states until they have had a few minutes to search. However, this is a pronunciation/transcription exercise, not a geography exercise, so hints such as the states should be given sometime.

Answers

State	Capital	Pronunciation
Alaska	Juneau	dʒuːnoʊ
Arizona	Phoenix	fiːnɪks
Colorado	Denver	denvər
Delaware	Dover	doʊvər
Georgia	Atlanta	ætlæntə
Idaho	Boise	bɔisi
Kansas	Topeka	toʊpiːkə
Maryland	Annapolis	ənæpəlɪs
Michigan	Lansing	lænsɪŋ
Montana	Helena	helɪnə
New Hampshire	Concord	kaːŋkɔːrd
New Mexico	Santa Fe	sæntə feɪ
New York	Albany	ɔːlbəni
North Carolina	Raleigh	rɑːli
North Dakota	Bismarck	bɪzmɑːrk
Ohio	Columbus	kəlʌmbəs
Oregon	Salem	seɪləm
South Dakota	Pierre	pɪr
Virginia	Richmond	rɪtʃmənd
Wyoming	Cheyenne	ʃaɪæn

Create your own: There are several websites that allow you to create your own wordsearches. However, they work with words in regular English spelling. In order to create a wordsearch in phonemic transcription:

- Decide what your words will be.
- Make sure you know how to transcribe them correctly.
- Devise a system for entering phonemic symbols that are not Roman alphabet letters. For example, the Roman alphabet letters *c*, *q*, *x*, and *y* are not used for English phonemic transcription, so they can be substituted for phonemic symbols such as ʃ, ŋ, ə, and ɔ.
- Use an online website to generate the wordsearch, for instance Discovery Education (n.d.).

You may still be able to add a word or two to the generated wordsearch, and generally tidy it up.

Worksheet

Find the names of 20 US state capital cities in this wordsearch. The names have been written in phonemic symbols. They may be horizontal, vertical or diagonal in any direction. To start you off, *Juneau*, the capital of Alaska, has been highlighted in the first row. If you are really stuck, the states are given underneath the puzzle as a clue.

æ	dʒ	uː	n	oʊ	m	z	r	ŋ	ɪ	tʃ	s
p	ɔː	l	b	ə	n	i	ə	ɪ	h	g	oʊ
v	uː	s	i	k	ə	l	v	s	r	ɪ	p
eɪ	d	ɪ	s	r	n	ɑː	oʊ	n	k	ɪ	k
f	n	l	ɔɪ	ɑː	ɪ	r	d	æ	ə	θ	ɑː
ə	ə	ə	b	m	l	æ	e	l	l	w	ŋ
t	m	p	s	z	e	t	n	f	ʌ	h	k
n	tʃ	æ	t	ɪ	h	l	v	iː	m	m	ɔː
æ	ɪ	n	l	b	dʒ	æ	ə	n	b	ə	r
s	r	ə	ʌ	l	tʃ	n	r	ɪ	ə	l	d
t	oʊ	p	iː	k	ə	t	f	k	s	eɪ	uː
n	æ	aɪ	ʃ	ə	t	ə	z	s	w	s	g

States

Alaska
Arizona
Colorado
Delaware
Georgia

Idaho
Kansas
Maryland
Michigan
Montana

New Hampshire
New Mexico
New York
North Carolina
North Dakota

Ohio
Oregon
South Dakota
Virginia
Wyoming

* This page is photocopiable for classroom use only.

D5

Let Us Prey

Pronunciation point: English has many homophones; that is, words that are pronounced the same but spelled differently. This shows that the spelling system of English is not very regular. Homophones do not occur, or are much less common, in other languages.

Minimum level: Intermediate

Exercise type: A matching game relying on memory (pelmanism), to be played in groups

Approximate time: 30 minutes (exercise), 10 minutes (debrief)

Preparation: Print out the 40 game cards below, preferably onto card rather than paper, and cut them up into individual cards. Make as many sets as you have groups of four or five learners in the class. For instance, for a class of 20, make four or five sets. On some cards, there is more than one transcription, for BrE and AmE pronunciations.

Introducing the exercise: Explain the concept of homophones.

Conducting the exercise:

- Divide the class into groups of four or five.
- Give each group a set of cards, shuffled. Tell the learners to lay them out into eight rows of five cards, face down.
- Explain that the blank cards are the first sentence, and the shaded cards are the second sentence, that follows on from the first to produce a joke.
- One by one, team members turn over two cards. If the two cards are the two parts of a joke, they keep the cards. If not, they turn them back over.
- The next member turns over two cards, and so on.
- The game continues until all the cards have been kept.

Debrief: Go through all 20 jokes, making sure the learners (i) understand the joke (some of the vocabulary is a little difficult), and (ii) can give the two possible spellings of the words given in phonemic transcription, i.e. homophones.

♦ 125

Game Cards

What do you call a piece of wood with nothing to do?	/bɔː(r)d/.	Why did the sheepdog fail his driving test?	Because he couldn't make a /juː/ turn.
What happens when a frog's car breaks down?	It gets /toʊd ~ təʊd/.	Where do you learn to greet people?	/haɪ/ school.
Why are Saturday and Sunday the strongest days of the week?	Because all the others are /wiːk/ days.	What happens if you sit on a grape?	It gives a little /waɪn/.
Why was the boy's school report card wet?	Because his grades were all below /siː/ level.	Why did the chicken cross the football pitch?	Because the referee shouted "/faʊl/!"
What fruit do socks prefer to eat?	/pɜrz ~ peəz/.	Did you hear about the vegetarian cannibal?	He only ate /swiːdz/.
Why should you not tell secrets to peacocks?	Because they are always spreading /teɪlz/.	Why did the girl run away from the dark castle?	She was afraid of the /naɪt/.
Waiter: /jɔː(r)/ sweet, sir.	Customer: Thank you. You're cute, too.	Waiter: It's /biːn/ soup, sir.	Customer: What is it now?
The magician didn't pull a rabbit out of his hat.	It was a /hɜr ~ heə/.	Why are libraries so tall?	Because they have lots of /stɔːrɪz/.
What did the fish say when it hit a concrete wall?	/dæm/!	Where do you learn to make ice cream?	At /sʌndeɪ/ school/.
What do lions say before they go out hunting for food?	Let us /preɪ/.	Why did the window go to see the doctor?	It was having /peɪnz/.

126 ◆ Spelling and Phonemic Symbols

D6

Never a Cross Word

Pronunciation point: The purpose of this exercise is to get learners thinking in terms of sounds, regardless of spellings. This crossword works in both AmE and BrE, although the transcriptions used may be slightly different, as shown in the Answers section below.

Minimum level: Two crosswords are given, one at elementary level, and the other at intermediate (because of the vocabulary level required)

Exercise type: A crossword, to be completed individually, in pairs, or groups, depending on the learners

Approximate time: 15 minutes (exercise), 30 minutes (debrief)

Preparation: Make one copy of the worksheet for each learner.

Also make sure the learners know the phonemic symbols. If necessary, show a list on the board/screen.

Introducing the exercise: Confirm that the learners understand the concept and rules of a crossword. They occur in most languages, even those that do not use an alphabetic writing system.

Conducting the exercise: Distribute or show the blank crossword and clues. Emphasize to the class that the answers use phonemic symbols, not letters in spelling. So, learners need to concentrate on the sounds in the pronunciation.

Debrief notes:

Answers

Elementary

Across

1 *think* /θɪŋk/, 3 *school* /skuːl/, 5 *ram* /ræm/, 6 *twin* /twɪn/, 8 *left* /left/, 10 *globe* /gloʊb ~ gləʊb/, 12 *child* /tʃaɪld/, 14 *mean* /miːn/, 15 *names* /neɪmz/, 16 *jump* /dʒʌmp/.

Down

1 *throat* /θroʊt ~ θrəʊt/, 2 *crown* /kraʊn/, 3 *smile* /smaɪl/, 4 *last* /læst ~ lɑːst/, 7 *wool* /wʊl/, 9 *fill* /fɪl/, 10 *green* /ɡriːn/, 11 *bombs* /bɑːmz ~ bɒmz/, 12 *change* /tʃeɪndʒ/, 13 *drop* /drɑːp ~ drɒp/.

Intermediate

Across

1 *focus* /foʊkəs ~ fəʊkəs/, 4 *bumps* /bʌmps/, 7 *cable* /keɪbəl/, 8 *exam* /ɪɡzæm/, 9 *ink* /ɪŋk/, 10 *toning* /təʊnɪŋ/, 12 *season* /siːzən/, 14 *coasts* /koʊsts ~ kəʊsts/, 17 *insane* /ɪnseɪn/, 20 *its* /ɪts/, 21 *bullock* /bʊlək/, 22 *canal* /kənæl/, 23 *beneath* /bɪniːθ/, 24 *passage* /pæsɪdʒ/

Down

1 *fixed* /fɪkst/, 2 *cabin* /kæbɪn/, 3 *sailing* /seɪlɪŋ/, 4 *bricks* /brɪks/, 5 *mazes* /meɪzɪz/, 6 *salmon* /sæmən/, 11 *oboe* /oʊboʊ ~ əʊbəʊ/, 13 *away* /əweɪ/, 14 *kebab* /kəbɑːb ~ kəbæb/, 15 *Ceylon* /sɪlɑːn ~ sɪlɒn/, 16 *sixth* /sɪksθ/, 17 *escape* /ɪskeɪp/, 18 *saints* /seɪnts/, 19 *knowledge* /nɑːlɪdʒ ~ nɒlɪdʒ/.

Worksheet 1

This crossword follows the normal rules of crosswords, except that the answers have to be written in phonemic symbols, not regular spelling. So, you must concentrate on the pronunciation.

Across

1. "I don't . . . John heard me."
3. Where your teachers teach you.
5. A male sheep.
6. One of two babies born at the same time.
8. The opposite of *right*.
10. A 3D model of the Earth.
12. "She has no brothers or sisters. She is an only . . ."
14. "What does this word . . . ?"
15. Smith, Brown and Jones are common English family . . .
16. "Basketball players can . . . high."

Down

1. The front part of your neck.
2. What a king or queen wears on their head.

* This page is photocopiable for classroom use only.

3 You . . . to show you are happy.
4 "I went to the cinema . . . night."
7 The hair of a sheep that you can knit into a jumper.
9 " . . . the saucepan with water, and boil it."
10 "We bought red and . . . apples."
11 Explosives dropped by an air force.
12 The Earth is getting warmer because of climate . . .
13 "Be careful! Don't . . . the glasses."

* This page is photocopiable for classroom use only.

Worksheet 2

This crossword follows the normal rules of crosswords, except that the answers have to be written in phonemic symbols, not regular spelling. So, you must concentrate on the pronunciation.

Across

1. Move a camera lens to get a clear, sharp picture
4. Raised parts of a surface, e.g. a road
7. What you use to connect parts of your computer, e.g. CPU, monitor, printer
8. "What mark did you get in your . . . ?"
9. Liquid, usually black, used for writing and printing
10. He is . . . his muscles by going to the gym every day
12. Summer is a . . .
14. The Atlantic and the Pacific are the two main . . . of the USA
17. The central city has . . . rental prices.
20. Belonging to something
21. An ox, a cow that cannot breed
22. A manmade waterway

* This page is photocopiable for classroom use only.

23 Under
24 A short piece of writing or music that is part of a larger work

Down

1 Firmly fastened
2 A bedroom on a ship
3 If something is easy to do, it is plain . . . (idiom)
4 Lego sets consist mostly of . . .
5 Children's games on paper, in which you try to draw a line through a complicated set of lines without crossing them
6 An edible fish with pink flesh
11 A woodwind instrument in a classical western orchestra
13 "Go . . . and leave me alone!"
14 Turkish-style meat and vegetables cooked on a stick
15 The former name of Sri Lanka
16 June is the . . . month of the year
17 The prisoner made a daring . . .
18 George, Andrew, David, and Patrick are the patron . . . of England, Scotland, Wales, and Ireland.
19 Information you have gained through learning or experience

* This page is photocopiable for classroom use only.

Section E
Vowels and Consonants

E1
Sounds in Common

Pronunciation point: In order to pronounce English words correctly, learners need to be able to keep pronunciations and spellings separate, and not be misled by the spellings. This exercise works in both AmE and BrE, although the pronunciations used may be slightly different, as shown in the Answers section below.

Minimum level: Two exercises are given, one at elementary level, and the other at intermediate (because of the vocabulary assumed).

Exercise type: A pen-and-paper exercise involving pronouncing out loud and thinking about sounds. It can be conducted individually or in pairs.

Approximate time: 15 minutes (exercise), 15 minutes (debrief)

Preparation: Make one copy of the worksheet for each learner. Alternatively, to save paper, either make the worksheet accessible in soft copy on learners' devices, or show the worksheet on a screen.

Introducing the exercise: Explain that the spelling system of English is probably less regular than that of the learners' own native languages. Illustrate this by using a few simple homophones (e.g. *hear, here*) and homographs (e.g. *wind*: "breeze," "turn") (see exercise D2); homophones and homographs probably do not exist in the learners' languages.

Conducting the exercise: The learners read the pairs of words, say them out loud, and work out which sound each pair has in common. Perhaps clarify this by working through the first one or two.

Debrief notes: Emphasize that English spelling can be a misleading indicator of the sounds in words. With more advanced learners, you could ask them to transcribe the words.

Answers

#	Words	Sound in common	Transcriptions
1	*soup, true*	/uː/	/suːp, truː/
2	*chemist, bank*	/k/	/kemɪst, bæŋk/

#	Words	Sound in common	Transcriptions
3	*wished, better*	/t/	/wɪʃt, betə(r)/
4	*flight, mine*	/aɪ/	/flaɪt, maɪn/
5	*gaming, hammer*	/m/	/ɡeɪmɪŋ, hæmə(r)/
6	*taxi, less*	/s/	/tæksi, les/
7	*anyone, best*	/e/	/enɪwʌn, best/
8	*parachute, English*	/ʃ/	/pærəʃuːt, ɪŋglɪʃ/
9	*physics, rough*	/f/	/fɪzɪks, rʌf/
10	*feather, wedding*	/e/	/feðə(r), wedɪŋ/
11	*cheetah, helped*	/t/	/tʃiːtə, helpt/
12	*become, young*	/ʌ/	/bɪkʌm, jʌŋ/
13	*zoom, praise*	/z/	/zuːm, preɪz/
14	*debt, brand*	/d/	/det, brænd/
15	*machine, breathe*	/iː/	/məʃiːn, briːð/
16	*guard, single*	/g/	/gɑː(r)d, sɪŋɡəl/
17	*ceiling, grass*	/s/	/siːlɪŋ, græs ~ grɑːs/
18	*rhythm, stitch*	/ɪ/	/rɪðəm, stɪtʃ/
19	*queen, southwest*	/w/	/kwiːn, saʊθwest/
20	*Matthew, yourself*	/j/	/mæθjuː, jɔː(r)self/
1	*piece, Beatles*	/iː/	/piːs, biːtəlz/
2	*design, cheese*	/z/	/dɪzaɪn, tʃiːz/
3	*worth, squeeze*	/w/	/wɜː(r)θ, skwiːz/
4	*prove, juice*	/uː/	/pruːv, dʒuːs/
5	*passion, cliché*	/ʃ/	/pæʃən, kliːʃeɪ/
6	*doubt, brushed*	/t/	/daʊt, brʌʃt/
7	*many, threat*	/e/	/meni, θret/
8	*lawless, proceed*	/s/	/lɔːlɪs, prəsiːd/
9	*rehearse, whose*	/h/	/rɪhɜː(r)s, huːz/
10	*yacht, disuse*	/j/	/jɑːt ~ jɒt, dɪsjuːs/
11	*bullet, unhook*	/ʊ/	/bʊlɪt, ʌnhʊk/
12	*laughter, suffix*	/f/	/læftər ~ lɑːftə, sʌfɪks/
13	*income, strong*	/ŋ/	/ɪŋkəm, strɔːŋ ~ strɒŋ/
14	*business, hymn*	/ɪ/	/bɪznɪs, hɪm/
15	*Judith, hedge*	/dʒ/	/dʒuːdɪθ, hedʒ/
16	*kingdom, Gwyneth*	/ɪ/	/kɪŋdəm, gwɪnɪθ/
17	*language, reservoir*	/w/	/læŋgwɪdʒ, rezə(r)vwɑː(r)/

#	Words	Sound in common	Transcriptions
18	*hated, break*	/eɪ/	/heɪtɪd, breɪk/
19	*reflex, once*	/s/	/riːfleks, wʌns/
20	*police, grieving*	/iː/	/pəliːs, griːvɪŋ/

Create your own materials: It is easy to create your own version, provided you are fairly familiar with sounds and phonemic symbols. You can concentrate on sounds that your learners mix up.

Worksheet 1

In each pair of words, only one sound occurs in both words. Say the words out loud, and work out the sound they share.

    Words   Sound in common (as a phonemic symbol)

1. *soup, true*
2. *chemist, bank*
3. *wished, better*
4. *flight, mine*
5. *gaming, hammer*
6. *taxi, less*
7. *anyone, best*
8. *parachute, English*
9. *physics, rough*
10. *feather, wedding*
11. *cheetah, helped*
12. *become, young*
13. *zoom, praise*
14. *debt, brand*
15. *machine, breathe*
16. *guard, single*
17. *ceiling, grass*
18. *rhythm, stitch*
19. *queen, southwest*
20. *Matthew, yourself*

* This page is photocopiable for classroom use only.

Worksheet 2

In each pair of words, only one sound occurs in both words. Say the words out loud, and work out the sound they share.

Words   Sound in common (as a phonemic symbol)

1 *piece, Beatles*
2 *design, cheese*
3 *worth, squeeze*
4 *prove, juice*
5 *passion, cliché*
6 *doubt, brushed*
7 *many, threat*
8 *lawless, proceed*
9 *rehearse, whose*
10 *yacht, disuse*
11 *bullet, unhook*
12 *laughter, suffix*
13 *income, strength*
14 *business, hymn*
15 *Judith, hedge*
16 *kingdom, Gwyneth*
17 *language, reservoir*
18 *hated, break*
19 *reflex, once*
20 *police, grieving*

* This page is photocopiable for classroom use only.

E2

What's the Difference?

Pronunciation point: Minimal pairs are pairs of words that differ only in that one word has one sound where the other word has a different sound, the rest remaining the same. Since we are talking about sounds, the spelling is irrelevant. Learners should not be misled by the spelling.

Minimum level: Intermediate (because of the vocabulary level implied)

Exercise type: A pen-and-paper exercise requiring a lot of thought about sounds. It can be conducted individually or in pairs.

Approximate time: 20 minutes (exercise), 15 minutes (debrief)

Preparation: Make one copy of the worksheet for each learner. Alternatively, to save paper, either make the worksheet accessible in soft copy on learners' devices, or show the worksheet on a screen.

Introducing the exercise: Introduce the concept of minimal pairs. Start with simple pairs, e.g. *bet, bat*, where the spelling closely reflects the pronunciation, and the distinguishing sound is clear. Then progress to more complex examples, e.g. *sheet, chute*, where the spelling is less of a clue. Emphasize that minimal pairs relate to sounds, not to spelling.

Conducting the exercise: Go through the first example (*feel, Phil*) with the class. Point out that it is sounds that are important here. Some of the examples relate to differences in vowel sounds, and some to consonants. Encourage learners to say the words out loud. Then it should be more obvious what difference there is in the pronunciation.

Answers

	Words	Different sounds
1	*feel, Phil*	/iː, ɪ/
2	*debt, death*	/t, θ/

	Words	Different sounds
3	*Dan, done*	/æ, ʌ/
4	*sue, zoo*	/s, z/
5	*lentil, rental*	/l, r/
6	*ballot, ballad*	/t, d/
7	*look, Luke*	/ʊ, u:/
8	*chateau, shadow*	/t, d/
9	*ankle, uncle*	/æ, ʌ/
10	*simple, symbol*	/p, b/
11	*false, falls*	/s, z/
12	*Max, mucks*	/æ, ʌ/
13	*streaked, strict*	/i:, ɪ/
14	*maternity, modernity*	/t, d/
15	*candle, Kendal*	/æ, e/
16	*taught, thought*	/t, θ/
17	*hood, who'd*	/ʊ, u:/
18	*precedent, president*	/s, z/
19	*calorie, gallery*	/k, g/
20	*salmon, summon*	/æ, ʌ/
21	*anchor, anger*	/k, g/
22	*Alice, alleys*	/s, z/
23	*scheme, skim*	/i:, ɪ/
24	*incite, inside*	/t, d/
25	*rice, rise*	/s, z/
26	*fanatic, phonetic*	/æ, e/
27	*Mauritius, malicious*	/r, l/
28	*cute, queued*	/t, d/
29	*Caesar's, scissors*	/i:, ɪ/
30	*oppressed, abreast*	/p, b/

Debriefing note: All the example words used work regardless of whether a BrE or AmE pronunciation is used. The pairs of sounds are ones that are often not distinguished by learners. The mistakes that learners make may reflect (i) features of their pronunciation, and (ii) the fact that they are misled by the spelling.

You could spend some time discussing the spelling correspondences of English sounds.

Create your own materials: This exercise has used somewhat advanced words with potentially misleading spelling. For learners at lower levels, use simpler, and less irregularly spelled, words. For minimal pairs for BrE pronunciation, see Higgins (2017).

Worksheet

The following pairs of words may look fairly different in their spelling, but in fact there is only one difference in their pronunciation. One word has a sound, where the other word has a different sound. Identify those sounds, by using their phonemic symbols.

	Words	Different sounds
1	feel, Phil	/iː, ɪ/
2	debt, death	
3	Dan, done	
4	sue, zoo	
5	lentil, rental	
6	ballot, ballad	
7	look, Luke	
8	chateau, shadow	
9	ankle, uncle	
10	simple, symbol	
11	false, falls	
12	Max, mucks	
13	streaked, strict	
14	maternity, modernity	
15	candle, Kendal	
16	taught, thought	
17	hood, who'd	
18	precedent, president	
19	calorie, gallery	
20	salmon, summon	
21	anchor, anger	
22	Alice, alleys	
23	scheme, skim	
24	incite, inside	
25	rice, rise	
26	fanatic, phonetic	
27	Mauritius, malicious	
28	cute, queued	
29	Caesar's, scissors	
30	oppressed, abreast	

* This page is photocopiable for classroom use only.

E3
Allan or Ellen?

Pronunciation point: Learners cannot be expected to pronounce words correctly if they do not know which sounds make up the words; that is, what their target sounds are. Often, but not always, this can be deduced from the spelling.

Minimum level: Two sample exercises are given, one at elementary level, the other at intermediate level. The exercise is exactly the same (searching for words that contain the /æ/ sound). The only difference is in the level of vocabulary assumed.

Exercise type: A maze-type recognition exercise, best conducted individually. It can be made into a race, to see who finishes first.

Approximate time: 5 minutes (exercise), 20 minutes (debrief)

Preparation: Make one copy of the worksheet for each learner. Alternatively, to save paper, either make the worksheet accessible in soft copy on learners' devices, or show the worksheet on a screen.

Introducing the exercise: Recap the /æ/ sound, to make sure the learners understand which vowel they are trying to identify.

Conducting the exercise: Learners identify, as quickly as possible, which route through the web contains /æ/ words. It can be made into a race, to see who finishes first.

Answers: The only route is:

>   (Elementary) *bad, flash, pack, land, crash, bag, track, gas, drank, mad, slapped, damp, Brad, Dad, pan, trapped.*
>   (Intermediate) *stamp, sacked, campus, bland, Sam, cattle, slam, badge, fancies, ramp, access, fanfare, mallow, barrel, mansion, trapped.*

Debriefing note: It may not be obvious, but the words were chosen because they have minimal pairs with words with other sounds that /æ/ is often confused with, namely /e/ and /ʌ/. Most /ɑː/ examples involve a following /r/ in AmE; they have mostly been omitted here, although they are minimal pairs (without the /r/) in BrE.

> (Elementary) *bad, bed, bud; flash, flesh, flush; pack, peck, puck; land, lend; crash, crush; bag, beg, bug; track, trek, truck; gas, guess, Gus; drank, drunk; mad, mud; slapped, slept; damp, dump; Brad, bread; Dad, dead, dud; pan, pen, pun; Ellen, Allen; any, Annie; X, ax; bets, bats, butts; letter, latter; pet, pat, putt; send, sand; palm, Pam; uncle, ankle; cup, cap; dumb, dam; drug, drag, dreg; lump, lamp; puddle, paddle, pedal/peddle.*
> (Intermediate) *bland, blend; Kendal, candle; cattle, kettle; phonetic, fanatic; fancies, fences; neck, knack; melody, malady; mallow, mellow; mansion, mention; access, excess; wreck, rack, ruck; sacked, sect, sucked; celery, salary; barrel, Beryl; calm, cam, come; Sam, psalm, some/sum; buggy, baggy; butter, better, batter; badge, budge; brush, brash; campus, compass; sucks, sacks/sax, sex; fanfare, funfair; mutter, matter; ramp, rump; salmon, summon; slam, slum; snug, snag; stamp, stump; thrush, thrash, thresh.*

You can therefore spend some time cementing the difference between these vowels by practicing the pronunciation of these minimal pair words.

You can also elicit the spelling patterns of these vowel sounds. The following percentages, using BrE, come from Carney (1994).

- /æ/ is spelled *a* (virtually 100% of the time).
- /e/ is spelled *e* 84% of the time (e.g. *ten*), *ea* 6% (e.g. *dead*), and various other spellings 9% (e.g. *bury*). There are only two words where *a* = /e/: *any* and *many*.
- /ɑː/ is spelled *ar* 60% (e.g. *park*) (and pronounced with an /r/ sound in AmE), *a* 34% (e.g. *father*), and other spellings 6%.
- /ʌ/ is spelled *u* 63% (e.g. *mud*), *o* 27% (e.g. *ton*), *ou* 8% (e.g. *touch*), and others 2%.

Create your own: it is in fact quite simple to produce such a maze-type game.

1. Decide which vowel sound you want to concentrate on.
2. Work out which other vowel sounds your learners often confuse this vowel sound with.
3. While you do not need to find minimal pairs in order to create this maze, minimal pairs are very useful in the debrief when discussing mistakes the learners have made. A very useful list of minimal pairs in English is Higgins (2017). While his lists use BrE pronunciation as

the reference, most of the words apply in AmE as well; check this. Make sure the words are at the right vocabulary level for the learners.
4. Use a format such as the spider's web used here. Enter the target words, making sure there is only one correct answer/route. Then add the other, distractor words.

Worksheet 1

You are the spider. Make your way to the center of the web by passing through only those words containing the /æ/ vowel (such as *bad* and *trapped* /bæd, træpt/).

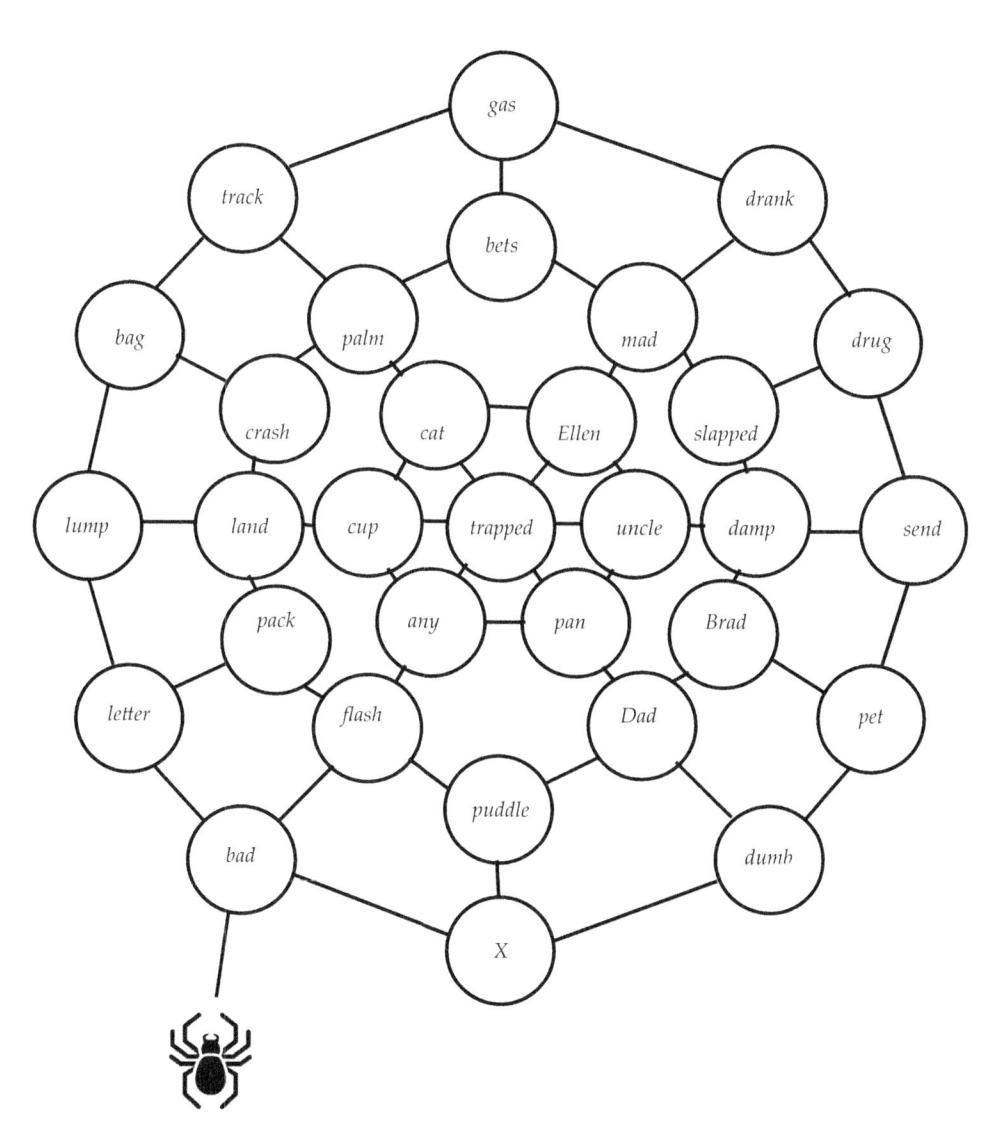

*This page is photocopiable for classroom use only.

Allan or Ellen? ◆ 147

Worksheet 2

You are the spider. Make your way to the center of the web by passing through only those words containing the /æ/ vowel (such as *stamp* and *trapped* /stæmp, træpt/).

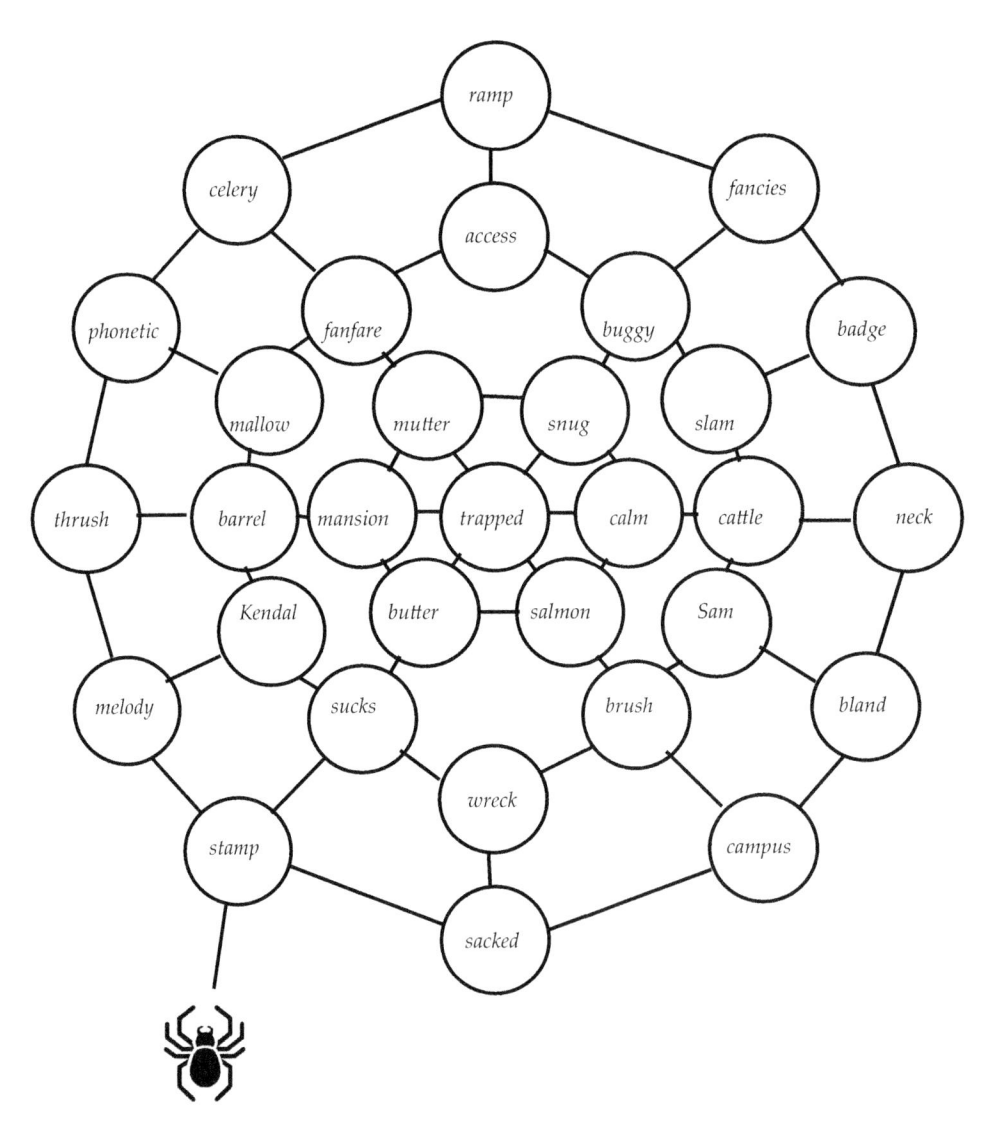

spider web diagram with words:

ramp, celery, fancies, access, phonetic, fanfare, buggy, badge, mallow, mutter, snug, slam, thrush, barrel, mansion, trapped, calm, cattle, neck, Kendal, butter, salmon, Sam, melody, sucks, brush, bland, wreck, campus, stamp, sacked

* This page is photocopiable for classroom use only.

148 ◆ Vowels and Consonants

E4

Do We Invite Yvonne?

Pronunciation point: Learners cannot be expected to pronounce words correctly if they do not know which sounds make up the words; that is, what their target sounds are. Often, but not always, this can be deduced from the spelling.

Minimum level: Intermediate

Exercise type: An individual exercise, checking whether names contain the /ɪ/ vowel

Approximate time: 20 minutes (exercise), 5 minutes (debrief)

Preparation: Make one copy of the worksheet for each learner. Alternatively, to save paper, either make the worksheet accessible in soft copy on learners' devices, or show the worksheet on a screen.

Introducing the exercise: Illustrate the /ɪ/ sound, for example with the word *indistinct* /ɪndɪstɪŋkt/.

Conducting the exercise: Learners identify which of the names contain the /ɪ/ vowel.

Debrief notes: The following names do contain the /ɪ/ vowel: *Bill, Chris, Crystal, Cynthia, Dick, Dylan, Evelyn, Gwyneth, Jim, Liz, Lynn, Phyllis, Robyn, Sid, Tim, Yvonne.*

This vowel is spelled with *i* 61% of the time (*bit*), *y* 20% (*rhythm*), and *e* in unstressed syllables 16% (*become*). However, these letters may represent other vowel sounds in English. Names that are examples of these various spelling-sound correspondences are used in this exercise.

Many of these names form minimal pairs with other words with the /iː, eɪ, e/ vowels, with which /ɪ/ is often confused, e.g. *Lynn, lean, lane, Len; Wayne, wean, win, when.*

Create your own materials: This kind of sound recognition exercise is easy to create. Determine the sound(s) that your learners find difficult, or that they confuse with other sounds. Then, perhaps using Higgins (2017), prepare a list of words, some using the sound, and some using the confusable sounds.

Worksheet

You are holding a party, but only want to invite people whose names contain the /ɪ/ vowel. Here is the total list of possible people. Which ones will you invite, i.e. which ones' names contain the /ɪ/ vowel?

Party invitation list

Invite? ✓ or ✗

❏ Bill	❏ Guy	❏ Pete
❏ Brian	❏ Gwyneth	❏ Phyllis
❏ Chris	❏ Jane	❏ Raymond
❏ Clive	❏ Jim	❏ Reg
❏ Crystal	❏ Keith	❏ Robyn
❏ Cynthia	❏ Kendal	❏ Ryan
❏ Dave	❏ Kylie	❏ Sid
❏ Diana	❏ Liz	❏ Tim
❏ Dick	❏ Lynn	❏ Tyrone
❏ Dylan	❏ Michael	❏ Wayne
❏ Evelyn	❏ Neil	❏ Wendy
❏ Fiona	❏ Penny	❏ Yvonne

* This page is photocopiable for classroom use only.

E5

United or Untied?

Pronunciation point: Learners from certain countries have problems pronouncing the /j/ sound of English. This may be because (i) it is not pronounced in their native language, and (ii) it is not reliably represented by any particular letters in English spelling.

Minimum level: Two exercises are given, at elementary and intermediate level. The difference is in the vocabulary used.

Exercise type: A maze, best conducted individually

Approximate time: 10 minutes (exercise), 10 minutes (debrief)

Preparation: Make one copy of the worksheet for each learner. Alternatively, to save paper, either make the worksheet accessible in soft copy on learners' devices, or show the worksheet on a screen.

Introducing the exercise: Illustrate the /j/ sound, for example with the word *yes*. Point out that, although it is often written with the letter y, and people may think of it as "the *y* sound," this is not a reliable clue (less than one fifth of the time; Carney, 1994, p. 255).

Conducting the exercise: Learners identify, as quickly as possible, which route through the maze contains /j/ words. They can move forwards or sideways, not diagonally. It can be made into a race, to see who finishes first.

Debrief notes:

Answers

> *use, yoga, few, cute, Europe, value, yellow, unique, review, music, year, barbecue, nephew, computer, amuse, onion, argue, your, unicorn*
> *beauty, uniform, young, yogurt, uranium, usual, stimulate, mule, yesterday, regular, volume, feud, ukulele, euthanasia, immunity, curious, canyon, funeral, utopia*

You might like to derive observations about the occurrence and spelling of /j/:

- It is not spelled with the letter *y* often (4% in terms of separate words, and 19% in terms of any text, i.e. taking into account how frequent those words are; Carney, 1994, p. 255).
- The digraph *ew* is pronounced /ju:/ (but see below).
- It often occurs before the /u:/ vowel sound spelled with the letter *u*. If the /u:/ vowel is spelled with oo, there is no /j/. This gives us pairs like *beauty/booty, feud/food, mute/moot* (Carney, 1994, p. 200).
- Words that begin with the *u* letter pronounced as /u:/ have the /j/ too, e.g. *united* (but not *untied*).

Most AmE speakers do not have /j/ after /θ, t, d, n, s, z/, e.g. *enthusiasm, tube, steward, duty, introduce, new, revenue, pseudo, pursue, Zeus, presume*. The /j/ is pronounced in BrE in these contexts. There are no examples of such words in this exercise.

Create your own materials: Like other exercises in this book, this is a maze format that can be used for many pronunciation features—not just sound recognition.

Worksheet 1

You are the mother T. Rex. Return to your nest by treading only in those adjacent footprints (horizontally or vertically, not diagonally) where the word contains the /j/ consonant, as in "You're huge!" /jɔː(r) hjuːdʒ/.

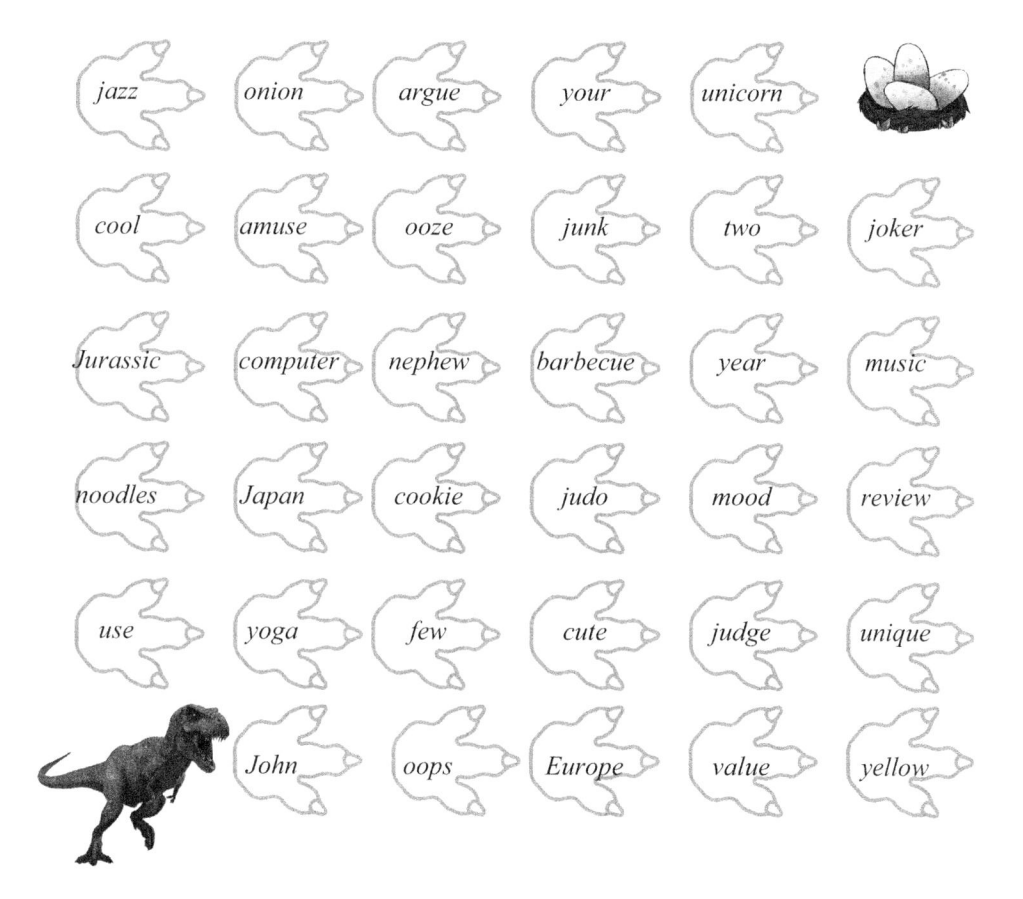

jazz	onion	argue	your	unicorn	🥚 (nest)
cool	amuse	ooze	junk	two	joker
Jurassic	computer	nephew	barbecue	year	music
noodles	Japan	cookie	judo	mood	review
use	yoga	few	cute	judge	unique
🦖	John	oops	Europe	value	yellow

* This page is photocopiable for classroom use only.

United or Untied? ◆ 153

Worksheet 2

You are the mother T. Rex. Return to your nest by treading only in those adjacent footprints (horizontally or vertically, not diagonally) where the word contains the /j/ consonant, as in "You're huge!" /jɔː(r) hjuːdʒ/.

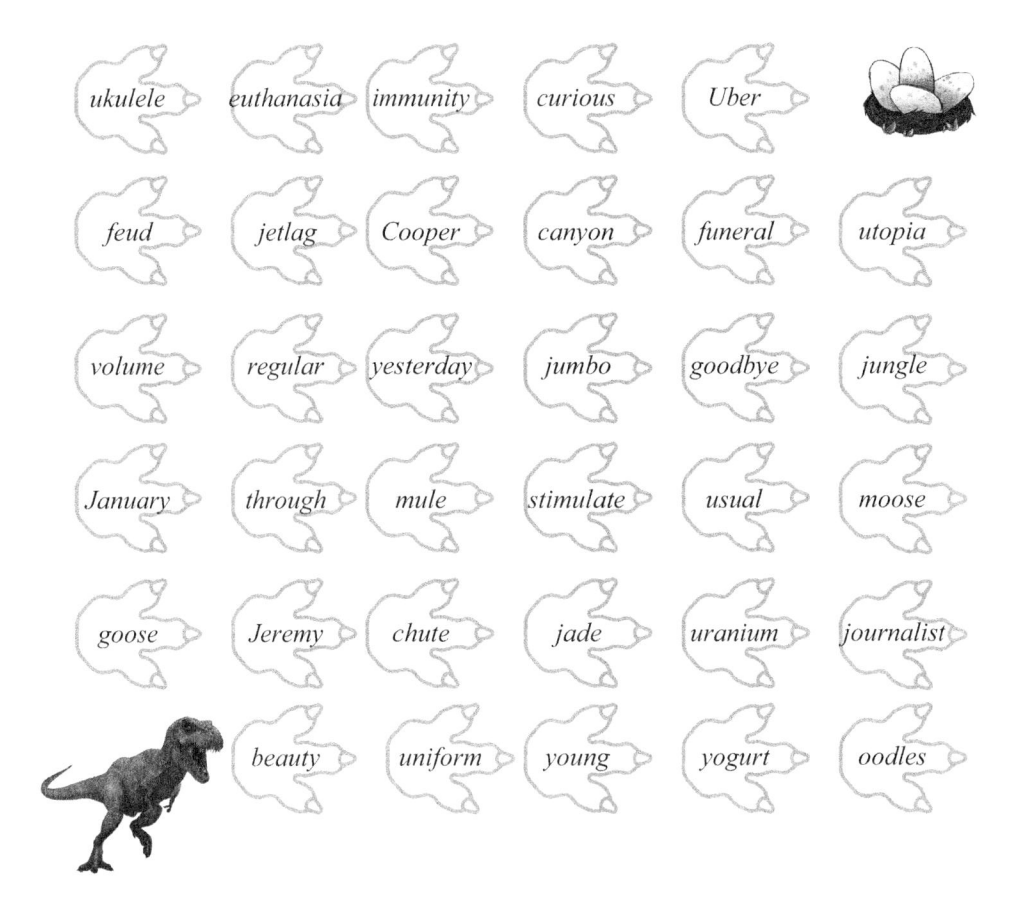

ukulele	euthanasia	immunity	curious	Uber	🥚 (nest)
feud	jetlag	Cooper	canyon	funeral	utopia
volume	regular	yesterday	jumbo	goodbye	jungle
January	through	mule	stimulate	usual	moose
goose	Jeremy	chute	jade	uranium	journalist
🦖	beauty	uniform	young	yogurt	oodles

* This page is photocopiable for classroom use only.

154 ◆ Vowels and Consonants

E6

Happy Hour

Pronunciation point: Learners cannot be expected to pronounce words correctly if they do not know which sounds make up the words; that is, what their target sounds are. Often, but not always, this can be deduced from the spelling.

Minimum level: Two sample exercises are given, one at elementary level, the other at intermediate level. The exercise is exactly the same (searching for words that contain the /h/ sound). The only difference is in the level of vocabulary assumed.

Exercise type: A maze-type recognition exercise, best conducted individually

Approximate time: 5 minutes (exercise), 20 minutes (debrief)

Preparation: Make one copy of the worksheet for each learner. Alternatively, to save paper, either make the worksheet accessible in soft copy on learners' devices, or show the worksheet on a screen.

Introducing the exercise: Recap the /h/ sound, to make sure the learners understand which consonant sound they are trying to identify. This is especially important for learners from languages like French and Spanish, that do not have the /h/ sound. Emphasize that they are looking for the /h/ sound, not the *h* letter; all the words in fact contain an *h* letter.

Conducting the exercise: Learners identify, as quickly as possible, which route through the clouds contains /h/ words. They can move forwards or sideways. It can be made into a race, to see who finishes first.

Answers: The only route is:

(Elementary) *happy, half, hello, hedge, manhood, who, Harry, keyhole, height, hotdog*

(Intermediate) *hippie, hostile, Hogwarts, rehearse, hybrid, whole, backhand, hospital, loophole, handsome.*

♦ 155

Debriefing note: Once the correct route has been found, get the learners to pronounce all the /h/ words. You could also ask them how the other words (without /h/) are pronounced. Eventually, you should arrive at the rule that, in English, /h/ only occurs at the beginning of a syllable. So, for example, two-syllable *manhood* is /mæn.hʊd/, where the "." shows the syllable division.

In terms of spelling correspondences:

- In a few words, it is spelled with *wh*: *who, whom, whose, whole, whooper, whore*.
- Otherwise, it is reliably spelled with the letter *h*.
- However, vice versa, the letter *h* may often be silent: *heir, honest, honor, hour, oh, yeah, pharaoh*.
- The letter *h* combines with several other letters to form digraphs (two letters representing one sound): *chest, phone, shirt, thirty, wheel*.

Create your own materials: Again, this is a maze format that can be used for many pronunciation features—not just sound recognition.

Worksheet 1

You are flying the plane. Make your way to the airport by passing through only those words containing the /h/ consonant sound (such as *hug* and *happy* /hʌg, hæpi/).

fish — what — hotdog — hand

rich — keyhole — height — rhythm — helmet

Harry — vehicle — stomach — Deborah

dough — who — manhood — hedge — rhino

cheetah — stomach — honest — hello

school — rhyme — ghost — earth — half

hour — hug — teach — happy

* This page is photocopiable for classroom use only.

Worksheet 2

You are flying the plane. Make your way to the airport by passing through only those words containing the /h/ consonant sound (such as *hug* and *happy* /hʌg, hæpi/).

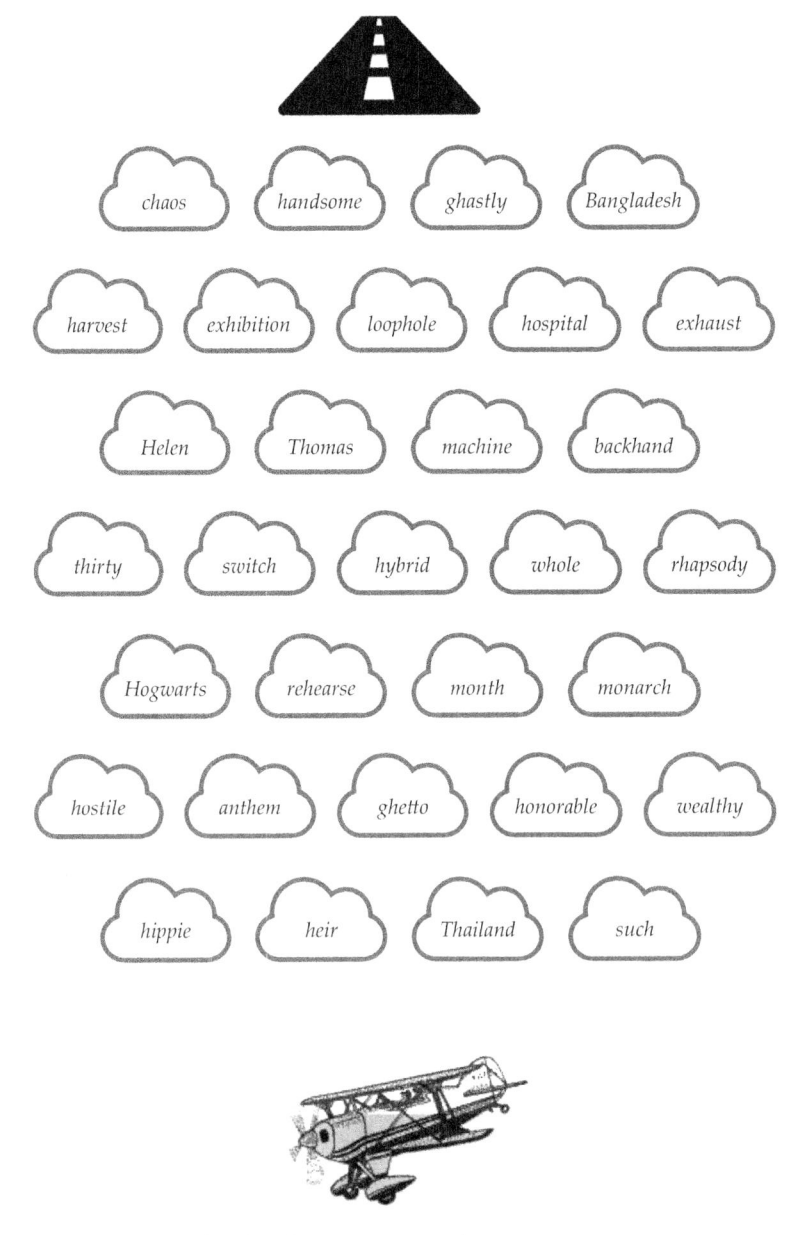

chaos *handsome* *ghastly* *Bangladesh*

harvest *exhibition* *loophole* *hospital* *exhaust*

Helen *Thomas* *machine* *backhand*

thirty *switch* *hybrid* *whole* *rhapsody*

Hogwarts *rehearse* *month* *monarch*

hostile *anthem* *ghetto* *honorable* *wealthy*

hippie *heir* *Thailand* *such*

* This page is photocopiable for classroom use only.

E7

So, Do Go!

Pronunciation point: English spelling uses an alphabetic system, where the letters (*a, b, c*, etc.) represent consonant and vowel sounds. However, the English spelling system is probably the least consistent alphabetic system of languages of the world. Learners may therefore come from languages with much more regular letter-sound correspondences. That is, in their languages' spelling systems, *x, y, z* are pronounced /x, y, z/ regularly and, vice versa, /x, y, z/ are spelled *x, y, z* regularly. They may therefore carry over to English the expectation that words can be reliably pronounced from their spellings. As this exercise shows, that is not the case.

Minimum level: Elementary

Exercise type: A pen-and-paper exercise involving pronouncing out loud and thinking about sounds. It is best conducted individually, but can be conducted in pairs, depending on the learners.

Approximate time: 15 minutes (exercise), 15 minutes (debrief)

Preparation: Make one copy of the worksheet for each learner. Alternatively, to save paper, either make the worksheet accessible in soft copy on learners' devices, or show the worksheet on a screen.

Introducing the exercise: A fun way to introduce the fact that English spelling is not a reliable indicator of pronunciation is to use the following poem:

When the English tongue we speak,
Why is *break* not rhymed with *freak*?
Will you tell me why it's true
We say *sew* but likewise *few*?
And the maker of the verse
And think of *goose* and yet with *choose*.
Think of *comb, tomb,* and *bomb,*
Doll and *roll* or *home* and *some.*
Since *pay* is rhymed with *say,*
Why not *paid* with *said* I pray?

Cannot rhyme his *horse* with *worse*?
Beard is not the same as *heard*.
Cord is different from *word*.
Cow is cow but *low* is low.
Shoe is never rhymed with *foe*.
Think of *hose*, *dose*, and *lose*
Think of *blood*, *food*, and *good*.
Mould is not pronounced like *could*.
Wherefore *done*, but *gone* and *lone*—
Is there any reason known?
To sum up all, it seems to me
Sound and letters don't agree.

The origins of this poem are not conclusively known. It appeared in the Simplified Spelling Society newsletter of 1917, but may date back to the *Spectator* magazine of 1902. See the English Spelling Society (n.d.) for this and other example poems.

Conducting the exercise: Distribute or show the worksheet. Explain that in each row, two of the words have the same-sounding ending (they rhyme), while the third does not (it has a different vowel sound). Learners should tick the odd one out.

Debrief notes: The odd ones out are *whose, give, do, put, have, were, most, pull, glove, bear, blood, quay, flour, does, worm, pint, bury, height, canoe, laughter*. Notice that many of these are very common words of English; some of the commonest words have irregular spellings.

Create your own materials: Carney (1994) lists the spelling-to-sound correspondences of (British) English.

Worksheet

Each row below contains three words. Two of them have same-sounding endings; that is, they rhyme. The third one has a different-sounding ending, with a different vowel sound. Tick the odd one out.

1	❏ rose	❏ whose	❏ nose
2	❏ give	❏ alive	❏ five
3	❏ so	❏ go	❏ do
4	❏ put	❏ cut	❏ shut
5	❏ wave	❏ have	❏ shave
6	❏ mere	❏ here	❏ were
7	❏ lost	❏ most	❏ cost
8	❏ pull	❏ gull	❏ dull
9	❏ stove	❏ grove	❏ glove
10	❏ dear	❏ clear	❏ bear
11	❏ blood	❏ food	❏ mood
12	❏ stay	❏ quay	❏ play
13	❏ pour	❏ four	❏ flour
14	❏ does	❏ goes	❏ toes
15	❏ storm	❏ form	❏ worm
16	❏ mint	❏ pint	❏ hint
17	❏ fury	❏ jury	❏ bury
18	❏ height	❏ weight	❏ freight
19	❏ toe	❏ canoe	❏ foe
20	❏ laughter	❏ daughter	❏ slaughter

* This page is photocopiable for classroom use only.

E8
Who? When? Where?

Pronunciation point: English has many silent letters; that is, letters in the spelling that represent no sound in the pronunciation. This is often because the sounds were pronounced in earlier versions of English, but while the sound has disappeared, the letter remains.

Other languages have no—or far fewer—silent letters. In other words, their spelling systems are more regular.

Minimum level: Intermediate (because of the vocabulary level)

Exercise type: A sound recognition exercise. It is best conducted individually, but can be conducted in pairs, depending on the learners.

Approximate time: 10 minutes (exercise), 15 minutes (debrief)

Preparation: Make one copy of the worksheet for each learner. Alternatively, to save paper, either make the worksheet accessible in soft copy on learners' devices, or show the worksheet on a screen.

Introducing the exercise: Introduce the notion of silent letters in English with common words such as *bread, comb, sign, knife, damn, receipt, island, listen, guard, answer*, where the underlined letters are silent. In the exercise, all the silent letters are in initial position in the word.

Conducting the exercise: Individually or in pairs, learners identify which of the three words has a different beginning from the other two. For *hour* and *heir*, the silent *h* represents no initial consonant (an empty onset); they are thus homophones of *our* and *air*.

Debrief notes: The odd ones out are *psalm, white, kite, Peugeot, gash, house, who, perish, key, wing, hair, wolf*.

All the silent letters in this exercise are in initial position. The following lists are all the common words that, with their related words (*who, whose, whom,* etc.), pattern like the examples in the exercise:

gnarl, gnash, gnat, gnaw, gnome
heir, honest, honor, hour
knack, knead, knee, kneel, knew, knickers, knife, knight, knitting, knob, knock, knot, know, knuckle
pneumatic, pneumonia
psalm, pseudo, psyche, psychedelic, psychiatrist, psychic, psychology, psychosis
ptarmigan, pterodactyl
who, whole
wrack, wrap, wrath, wreath, wreck, wren, wrench, wrestling, wretched, wriggle, wring, wrinkle, wrist, write, wrong

Create your own materials: Carney (1994) lists the spelling-to-sound correspondences of (British) English.

The exercise can be extended by considering silent letters in non-initial position. There are many websites of silent letters in English on the internet.

Worksheet

In each of the following sets of three words, tick the word that starts with a different onset (consonant sound(s), or no consonants, before the vowel sound) from the other two.

1	❏ palm	❏ psalm	❏ Pam
2	❏ white	❏ write	❏ rite
3	❏ knight	❏ night	❏ kite
4	❏ Peugeot	❏ neurotic	❏ pneumatic
5	❏ gnash	❏ Nash	❏ gash
6	❏ hour	❏ house	❏ our
7	❏ who	❏ when	❏ where
8	❏ pterodactyl	❏ terrible	❏ perish
9	❏ key	❏ knee	❏ need
10	❏ wring	❏ wing	❏ ring
11	❏ air	❏ heir	❏ hair
12	❏ whole	❏ wolf	❏ hole

* This page is photocopiable for classroom use only.

E9–15 Communicative Minimal Pair Work

All the following exercises have the same format. The difference is in the sounds being contrasted. Whether you use the particular exercises given here depends on the particular segmental pronunciation problems your students have. If you have a class of fairly homogeneous students who can distinguish, say, /r/ and /l/ easily, quite possibly because the phonology of their native language distinguishes them, then that exercise (E12) is not needed. In a class of mixed nationalities, some students will have certain problems, while other students will have different ones. It is therefore a good idea to mix nationalities in the pairings. It may be that one learner who does make the distinction can coach the other learner, who may find it difficult.

Pronunciation point: See the individual exercises, where this is explained.

Minimum level: Elementary (although some vocabulary may need to be introduced)

Exercise type: Pairwork production and perception exercises

Approximate time: This varies depending on the exercise. Some exercises have more examples than others. Some exercises relate to sounds that particular students may find very difficult, while other students may pronounce and hear them easily.

Preparation: Make one copy of the sentence worksheet and one copy of the response worksheet for each learner. They could be printed back to back, so that the learner can only read either the stimuli (on one side) or the responses (on the other).

Introducing the exercise: See the individual exercises, where guidelines for introducing the pronunciation differences are given.

Conducting the exercise:

- Divide the class into pairs. Mix the nationalities, if possible and appropriate.
- Distribute the sentence and response worksheets.
- Explain that, for each item, one member of the pair (A) will be the speaker, and the other (B) the listener. So, A should not look at the response worksheet, and B should not look at the sentence worksheet. This forces the two members to listen carefully.
- A chooses either the first or the second sentence, e.g. "Did the shepherd take his pig?" and says it out loud to B. B listens carefully to what A says, and works out which of the two alternative responses makes sense as a response to the stimulus, in this case,

"Yes, and he sold it at market"—not "Yes, he chose the red tractor" (which would follow "Did the shepherd take his pick?").

- Provided A agrees that B's response makes sense as a response to the sentence, they go on to #2. If it is the wrong response, i.e. it does not make sense, this could be because (i) the speaker did not pronounce the sentence clearly enough, and/or (ii) the listener did not listen carefully enough. A and B should work out the problem.
- In each set of sentences, A could take the role of the speaker in the first half of the items, and B in the second half.

Debrief notes: One of the beauties of this exercise is that it emphasizes to the students that their classmates did not understand what they were saying. This may come as a shock to the students. This may even happen where the students are of the same nationality.

Create your own materials: It is not easy, but not impossible, to create your own versions. The particular segmental pronunciation problems of your students may not have been covered by the sample exercises given here. To create items, (i) find out the minimal pairs distinguished by your students' pronunciation problems (Higgins, 2017 is a good place to start, although it is for BrE pronunciation), (ii) create two identical sentences except for the minimal pair, (iii) create two alternative responses, where the first response works for one of the sentences and not the other, and vice versa.

Another variation would be not to allow the speaker to choose which sentence to pronounce; you may find that speakers choose the one that they know they can pronounce clearly. Instead, prepare a new sentence worksheet with only one sentence each time, alternating randomly between the two sounds; that is, for example, sentence 1 only contains the /r/ sentence, while sentence 2 only contains the /l/ sentence, and so on.

For the above reasons, these communicative pairwork exercises have an advantage over conventional minimal pair exercises, which are often little more than uncommunicative drills. A well-known saying in ELT circles is, "A drill is a device for boring."

E9
A Big Pig

Pronunciation point:

A major problem for some learners is distinguishing the so-called voiceless plosives /p, t, k/ from the so-called voiced ones /b, d, g/.

They are "so-called" because voicing is not usually the clearest signal to be focused on. Indeed, voiced plosives may often be virtually voiceless. There are three clearer signals.

Firstly, in syllable-initial position, the voiceless ones are usually released with a burst of voiceless air (aspiration), before the voicing for the following vowel starts up. Thus, there is aspiration in *pin*, but not in *bin*. A piece of paper or a feather held in front of the mouth makes this obvious.

Secondly, vowels preceding the voiceless set /p, t, k/ are shorter than those preceding the voiced set /b, d, g/. They do not become different vowels (e.g. long /iː/ does not become short /ɪ/), but are shorter versions. So, the vowel in *beat* is shorter than that in *bead*.

Finally, the phenomenon of linking should not be forgotten. If your learners have a tendency to drop final plosives, put them in contexts where the following word begins with a vowel sound, so that they can be linked, and not dropped, e.g. *swap it* versus *swab it*. In such contexts, the difference between voiced and voiceless may be more obvious.

Stimuli 1–10 relate to initial plosives; 11–20 to final plosives; and 21–25 to final plosives being dropped. Note that there are no examples of plosives in the middle of words, especially between vowels, because in AmE the voiceless /t/ is usually changed into the voiced /d/. Thus, *Plato* and *playdough* may be identical. This is known as intervocalic voicing (making something voiceless into voiced, between voiced vowels).

Worksheet

Sentences

1. Was the peach enjoyable?
   Was the beach enjoyable?

2. How big is your class?
   How big is your glass?

3. Where does this train go?
   Where does this drain go?

4. Is it pouring?
   It is boring?

5. Do you like tennis?
   Do you like Dennis?

6. Did you see the coast?
   Did you see the ghost?

7. How long was the pan?
   How long was the ban?

8. Did you hear that Greek?
   Did you hear that creak?

9. Did you try the blue sweater?
   Did you dry the blue sweater?

10. What was next to the path?
    What was next to the bath?

11. What's that, on your back?
    What's that, on your bag?

12. What is that rope made of?
    What is that robe made of?

13. Tell me where the boy hit the ball.
    Tell me where the boy hid the ball.

14. Did you buy some tacks at the stationery shop?
    Did you buy some tags at the stationery shop?

* This page is photocopiable for classroom use only.

15 Where did the taxi driver leave his cap?
   Where did the taxi driver leave his cab?

16 Are the stripes on your car white?
   Are the stripes on your car wide?

17 What's that, in the muck over there?
   What's that, in the mug over there?

18 Did you buy those wooden clocks in Amsterdam?
   Did you buy those wooden clogs in Amsterdam?

19 Why did the zookeeper examine the cup?
   Why did the zookeeper examine the cub?

20 How should I write to my grandmother?
   How should I ride to my grandmother?

21 What was in the picture?
   What was in the pitcher?

22 Did you mix your late-night drink?
   Did you miss your late-night drink?

23 My son has a problem with addiction.
   My son has a problem with addition.

24 Why is the box so big?
   Why is the boss so big?

25 Which section do the violinists belong to?
   Which session do the violinists belong to?

* This page is photocopiable for classroom use only.

Worksheet

Responses

1. It was delicious.
   No. It was crowded.

2. Not too large: 100 cc.
   Not too large: 16 students.

3. Manchester Central station.
   The sewer.

4. No. I find it really interesting.
   Yes. I've never seen such heavy rain.

5. No. I prefer badminton.
   Yes. He's a lovely man.

6. No. I don't believe in them.
   Yes. It's very beautiful.

7. Fifteen inches.
   Three years.

8. Yes, but I couldn't understand him.
   Yes. I think that floorboard is loose.

9. No. It really wasn't wet.
   Yes, but it didn't fit me.

10. A soap dish.
    A wire fence.

11. A tattoo.
    A New Zealand badge.

12. Toweling.
    Wire.

13. In his pocket.
    Through the window.

14. Yes, and I pinned up all the notices.
    Yes, and I tied them onto my luggage.

* This page is photocopiable for classroom use only.

15. Outside, with the engine running.
    On the dining table.

16. No. They're red.
    No. They're narrow.

17. Tea.
    A pig.

18. Yes, but the cuckoo's not working on this one.
    Yes, but they're very uncomfortable to wear.

19. Because it had broken its leg.
    To see if the handle was chipped.

20. Take an Uber taxi.
    Include some of our holiday photos.

21. Pepsi.
    A landscape.

22. Yes, it was delicious.
    Yes, I was thirsty later on.

23. Don't worry, lots of kids are poor at arithmetic.
    Oh dear, is he on drugs?

24. There's a washing machine inside.
    He eats too many business lunches.

25. The string section.
    The afternoon session.

* This page is photocopiable for classroom use only.

E10

I Sought; I Thought; I Taught

Pronunciation point:

There are three main pairs of sounds that learners confuse with /θ, ð/: /t, d/, /s, z/, /f, v/.

/θ, ð/ are dental fricatives. Dental means that the tongue sticks out between the teeth, but not very far. This means that learners can easily see the difference between /θ, ð/ (dental) and (i) /t, d, s, z/ (alveolar), where the tongue does not stick out, and (ii) /f, v/ (labio-dental), where it is the lower lip that moves, not the tongue. All this is clearly visible.

Fricative means that the tongue comes towards the upper teeth, without touching them, but leaving a small gap through which air passes, creating a hissing sound. Since air escapes, the sound can be prolonged. This distinguishes /θ, ð/ (fricatives) from /t, d/ (plosives), where there is contact, and once the contact is released, the sound ends, i.e. they are not prolongable.

Worksheet

Sentences

1. Why is your thigh so dirty?
   Why is your tie so dirty?

2. This sum is giving me pain.
   This thumb is giving me pain.

3. Boat trips to France are enjoyable.
   Both trips to France are enjoyable.

4. We held a tense meeting.
   We held a tenth meeting.

5. How did the general send his thanks?
   How did the general send his tanks?

6. I have free tickets to the Taylor Swift concert.
   I have three tickets to the Taylor Swift concert.

7. Why did you choose a new theme for the project?
   Why did you choose a new team for the project?

8. Fate brought my husband and me together.
   Faith brought my husband and me together.

9. Jane is really useful.
   Jane is really youthful.

10. The teacher thought that Man was descended from the apes.
    The teacher taught that Man was descended from the apes.

* This page is photocopiable for classroom use only.

Worksheet

Responses

1. It was in my soup.
   I've been playing football.

2. I hate arithmetic too.
   Did you hit it with the hammer?

3. But I get seasick.
   But I can only afford to go on one trip, not two.

4. Why? Did you not solve the problem in the first nine meetings?
   Why? Was everyone nervous that the company would be sold?

5. Overland.
   By fax.

6. Lucky you! They must be worth a lot of money.
   Who are the two other people you're going with?

7. Because the previous one couldn't get along together.
   Because the previous one had already been investigated.

8. You accidentally met him at a party, didn't you?
   You attended the same church, didn't you?

9. Yes, she knows so much about IT.
   Yes, how does she keep looking much younger than she really is?

10. But some biologists think otherwise.
    But that's not part of the syllabus!

* This page is photocopiable for classroom use only.

E11

Take the Dose, Then Doze

Pronunciation point:

As for the plosives (see E9), the main difference between voiceless /s/ and voiced /z/ is not usually voicing.

Being the voiceless member of the pair, /s/ usually has more hiss (frication) than the voiced member, /z/. The same is true of /f, v; θ, ð; ʃ, ʒ/.

As we saw with the plosives, the voiceless member in final position shortens the preceding vowel. Thus, *Bruce* is shorter than *brews*. The same is true of *leaf, leave; teeth, teethe; Confucian, confusion*. (In fact, there are very few minimal pairs for /θ, ð; ʃ, ʒ/ and for initial /s, z/.)

Worksheet

Sentences

1. Where can I get some peace?
   Where can I get some peas?

2. What did you think of the race?
   What did you think of the rays?

3. Did you buy the sink?
   Did you buy the zinc?

4. What's above the ice?
   What's above the eyes?

5. I fell on my niece.
   I fell on my knees.

6. Can you hear a bus?
   Can you hear a buzz?

7. The price was too much.
   The prize was too much.

8. What's the problem with the precedent?
   What's the problem with the president?

9. What did the vet do with the deceased dog?
   What did the vet do with the diseased dog?

10. Can you see the spice?
    Can you see the spies?

* This page is photocopiable for classroom use only.

Worksheet

Responses

1. The supermarket is still open.
   Try the library.

2. It was very fast.
   They were very bright.

3. Yes. It's stainless steel.
   Yes, and I'll fix it onto the roof tomorrow.

4. Eyebrows.
   Fishermen's huts.

5. Oh dear! Did you damage your kneecaps?
   Oh dear! Is she all right?

6. Yes. I think one's just round the corner.
   Don't worry. It's just my smartphone vibrating.

7. Yes. Jackpot winners usually waste what they win.
   Yes. You can buy it cheaper elsewhere.

8. Everyone will want to do it now.
   He intends to resign.

9. He buried it.
   He gave it an injection.

10. Of course not. They're hiding.
    Over there, in the rack.

* This page is photocopiable for classroom use only.

E12

Jerry Ate a Jelly

Pronunciation point: Learners from some native languages have problems with these two sounds, because they are not distinct sounds in their language. However, the distinction between the two can be important in English.

There are various points to note about these two English sounds:

- /r/ is probably the consonant sound with the most variation in English. That is, it can be pronounced in various different ways.
- Rhoticity refers to whether the /r/ sound can occur in syllable-final position, as in *car park*, or not. Accents of English that have this are called rhotic (AmE, and others such as Scottish and Irish), while those that do not are non-rhotic (the BrE accent used here, and others such as Australian and New Zealand).
- On the other hand, /l/ has little variation in pronunciation and occurrence.
- The main distinction in the pronunciation of /r/ and /l/ is that for /l/ the tongue tip touches the roof of the mouth (alveolar ridge), whereas in /r/ it does not (for most variations of /r/). This is something that is easy to feel.
- Another, minor difference is that /r/ often has some lip-rounding, while /l/ does not.
- One common feature of learner English (and of some native accents) is for this tongue contact to be lost, or for the /l/ to be dropped altogether. For example, *all* /ɔːl/ becomes *awe* /ɔː/. Sentence 10 (*rolled* versus *rowed*) is an example of this (for both AmE and BrE).

Putting together the points above, examples 3, 6, and 7 in the exercise (e.g. *temper* versus *temple*) give the following possibilities:

- For AmE classes, the distinction is between final /r/ and final /l/.
- For BrE classes, it is between final /l/ and no final consonant.

Worksheet

Sentences

1. What kind of sheep is a ram?
   What kind of sheep is a lamb?

2. How do you spell the girl's name *Irene*?
   How do you spell the girl's name *Eileen*?

3. Why did your mother go into a temper?
   Why did your mother go into a temple?

4. Did you use a red battery?
   Did you use a lead battery?

5. What happened after the pirate boarded the ship?
   What happened after the pilot boarded the ship?

6. Why was the patient's medical report stamped "Cancer"?
   Why was the patient's medical report stamped "Cancel"?

7. Do we need a litter bin?
   Do we need a little bin?

8. What did the teacher do after she corrected the homework?
   What did the teacher do after she collected the homework?

9. Is there a lot of royal support?
   Is there a lot of loyal support?

10. What did the crew do after they rowed the boat to the shore?
    What did the crew do after they rolled the boat to the shore?

* This page is photocopiable for classroom use only.

Worksheet

Responses

1. A young one.
   An adult male.

2. I, R, E, N, E
   E, I, L, E, E, N

3. Because my sister had taken her handbag.
   Because she wanted to pray.

4. No, I used a lithium one.
   No, I used a green one.

5. He killed the captain with his sword.
   He guided it safely into port.

6. Because he had been sent home.
   Because his lungs were infected with it.

7. Yes. There isn't much rubbish.
   Yes. There is a lot of rubbish.

8. She added up the total marks.
   She corrected it.

9. Yes, our local football team always gets large crowds.
   Yes, the Queen strongly approves of it.

10. They got out.
    They got in.

* This page is photocopiable for classroom use only.

E13

Caesar's Scissors

Pronunciation point:

This distinction ought to be easy for learners because it is exactly what it says it is: the long vowels /iː, ɑː/ are longer than the short vowels /ɪ, ʌ/. In terms of the quality of the sounds, as determined by the position of the tongue and lips, they are similar (but not identical).

There are three factors to consider:

Firstly, in many languages of the world, there is no clear distinction between long vowels and short vowels, all vowels being a similar length. Learners from these languages are therefore likely to need some readjustment for English.

Secondly, there is another distinction in length in English between vowels before voiceless consonants, and those before voiced consonants. We have already alluded to this in E9 and E11. However, while the vowel in *beat* is shorter than the vowel in *bead*, it is the same vowel sound (phoneme), and thus the same symbol: /biːt, biːd/. It is simply a long or short version (allophone) of the vowel (phoneme) /iː/. The vowel has not changed to the short phoneme /ɪ/ as in *bit* or *bid*.

Finally, there are four long versus short vowel pairs in English:

- /iː, ɪ/: These are distinguished in all major varieties of English, and there are plenty of minimal pairs. The first exercise below uses /iː, ɪ/ and can be used by all learners.
- /ɑː, ʌ/: These are distinguished in all major varieties of English. However, the /ɑː/ vowel is very often followed by /r/ in AmE and similar accents (known as rhotic): *car park* /kɑː pɑːk/ (BrE), /kɑːr pɑːrk/ (AmE). As a result, there are very few minimal pairs, because /ʌ/ is not similarly followed by /r/. An additional issue is that what is pronounced with /ɑː/ in BrE and similar accents is

often pronounced with /æ/ in AmE, e.g. *grant, graph, pass* /grænt, græf, pæs/ (AmE), /grɑːnt, grɑːf, pɑːs/ (BrE).
- /ɔː, ɒ/: These are a long and short pair in BrE, and thus like the above pairs. However, in AmE, /ɒ/ is often pronounced /ɑː/, as in *lot, dodge, possible, quality* /lɑːt, dɑːdʒ, pɑːsəbəl, kwɑːləti/.
- /uː, ʊ/: These are a long and short pair in AmE and BrE. However, some accents, notably Scottish, do not distinguish the two. Also, there are very few minimal pairs.

In light of the above points, there is a full exercise below for /iː, ɪ/, which any teacher can use. The exercise for /ɑː, ʌ/ can only be used by non-AmE teachers. There is also no exercise for /ɔː, ɒ/ or /uː, ʊ/. However, if learners master the /iː, ɪ/ distinction, we can expect them to also master the other distinctions since they are the same difference between long and short vowel phonemes.

Worksheet 1

Sentences

1 Why did he sleep on the floor?
   Why did he slip on the floor?

2 How long is a week?
   How long is a wick?

3 If you eat that peel, it might make you sick.
   If you eat that pill, it might make you sick.

4 I hear the boxer beat his opponent.
   I hear the boxer bit his opponent.

5 When did Muhammad leave?
   When did Muhammad live?

6 He's preparing the peach.
   He's preparing the pitch.

7 What kind of feeling do you have?
   What kind of filling do you have?

8 Were there many beads for the necklace?
   Were there many bids for the necklace?

9 It was a terrible scene.
   It was a terrible sin.

10 Did the high heels make her feet sore?
    Did the high hills make her feet sore?

* This page is photocopiable for classroom use only.

Worksheet 1

Responses

1. It was soapy.
   He found the bed uncomfortable.

2. Seven days, of course.
   Usually an inch or two.

3. But my doctor gave it to me!
   Nonsense! Oranges are good for you.

4. Yes, on the ear.
   Yes, he won the title.

5. My friend Muhammad left five minutes ago.
   Prophet Muhammad lived 570 to 632.

6. By mowing the grass?
   By peeling it?

7. I'm disgusted.
   My donut has strawberry inside.

8. Only one buyer was interested in it.
   Not enough to complete it.

9. Yes. The traffic accident left two people dead.
   Yes. He should go to prison.

10. Yes, she should wear lower ones.
    Yes, she should climb lower ones.

* This page is photocopiable for classroom use only.

Worksheet 2

Sentences

1. What do you find in barns normally?
   What do you find in buns normally?

2. Where did those tasks come from?
   Where did those tusks come from?

3. If you calm down, we can discuss your problem.
   If you come down, we can discuss your problem.

4. Why is that carp in the water?
   Why is that cup in the water?

5. Who wrote this psalm?
   Who wrote this sum?

6. There's a new drama for the group.
   There's a new drummer for the group.

7. Why is the staff still here?
   Why is the stuff still here?

8. I'm painting a picture of a park.
   I'm painting a picture of a puck.

* This page is photocopiable for classroom use only.

Worksheet 2

Responses

1. Cattle.
   Raisins.

2. They were imported illegally from Africa.
   My English workbook.

3. Why can't we discuss it up here?
   I am not angry!

4. They're trying to breed them.
   It needs washing. It's got lipstick on it.

5. The Prophet David.
   My arithmetic teacher.

6. He's very loud.
   It's a historical tragedy.

7. They are refusing to leave the office.
   I haven't thrown it out yet.

8. You'll need lots of black, then.
   You'll need lots of green, then.

* This page is photocopiable for classroom use only.

E14

We Are Phonetics Fanatics

Pronunciation point:

The two vowels contrasted here are both short vowels. The difference is in the tongue position, specifically tongue height. The one of the pair that typically causes problems is /æ/. For /æ/, the tongue is lower than for /e/; that is, the mouth is wider open. Also, the lips are drawn wide apart sideways.

Worksheet

Sentences

1. My cousin's name is Ellen.
   My cousin's name is Allan.

2. There's a band in the road.
   There's a bend in the road.

3. Why did he mark the tree with an X?
   Why did he mark the tree with an axe?

4. My father is dead.
   My father is "Dad."

5. What is the price of that gem?
   What is the price of that jam?

6. What was in the rack?
   What was in the wreck?

7. How much is your celery?
   How much is your salary?

8. Why did the cattle feel so hot?
   Why did the kettle feel so hot?

9. Why was Jim paddling so hard?
   Why was Jim pedaling so hard?

10. Which track did you like best?
    Which trek did you like best?

* This page is photocopiable for classroom use only.

Worksheet

Responses

1. I know. I've met him.
   I know. I've met her.

2. They're playing a march.
   Slow down—it's a sharp U-shaped bend.

3. To indicate that it was to be preserved.
   Because he couldn't find a penknife.

4. I call mine "Papa."
   Oh, I'm so sorry to hear that.

5. $5.
   $5,000.

6. Toast.
   Treasure.

7. $30,000.
   $3.

8. Some of them had a fever.
   It had just been boiled.

9. He was approaching a steep hill.
   There was a strong current in the river.

10. The one by Taylor Swift.
    The one in Nepal.

* This page is photocopiable for classroom use only.

E15

Pause, Then Pose for the Camera

Pronunciation point:

Diphthongs are vowel sounds whose quality changes because the tongue and/or lip position changes during the vowel. They are in contrast with monophthongs, where the tongue and lips stay relatively stable, and the vowel sounds the same throughout.

As a result, diphthongs are represented by two symbols in transcription (e.g. /eɪ/ in *pain*), whereas monophthongs have only one symbol (e.g. /e/ in *pen*). Diphthongs are long, while monophthongs can be long or short.

There is a lot of variation in the diphthong/monophthong distinction—and in vowel sounds generally—between accents of English. The vowels of *made* and *mode* are very diphthongal (involving a lot of change) in Australian accents, but largely monophthongal (with little movement) in Scottish accents. Because non-rhotic BrE accents do not pronounce an /r/ in *here, where, poor*, they have diphthongs instead: /hɪə, weə, pʊə/. For many of these accents, the vowel of *where* is a long monophthong rather than a diphthong.

For reasons like the aforementioned, it is difficult to give exercises that are widely applicable since it depends on the reference accent used for pronunciation teaching.

The exercise below covers the monophthong-diphthong distinctions /e, eɪ; ɔː, əʊ ~ oʊ; ɒ ~ ɑː, əʊ ~ oʊ/.

Worksheet

Sentences

1. Show me where the pen is.
   Show me where the pain is.

2. Why is Henry so bald?
   Why is Henry so bold?

3. My cousin's name is John.
   My cousin's name is Joan.

4. Could I borrow the pepper please?
   Could I borrow the paper please?

5. What did he do with the lawn?
   What did he do with the loan?

6. How big are wells, usually?
   How big are whales, usually?

7. Why do we need a new cot for the baby?
   Why do we need a new coat for the baby?

8. What was Jane sawing?
   What was Jane sewing?

9. When does he want to sell his boat?
   When does he want to sail his boat?

10. Who is the famous Paul you met at the party?
    Who is the famous Pole you met at the party?

* This page is photocopiable for classroom use only.

Worksheet

Responses

1. It's here in my shoulder.
   It's here in my briefcase.

2. His whole family have little hair.
   Yes. He's never been afraid of taking risks.

3. I know. I've met her.
   I know. I've met him.

4. Sure. The football results are on the back page.
   Sure. And here's the salt.

5. He put in a flower bed.
   He bought himself a car.

6. At least 20 feet long.
   At least 20 feet deep.

7. The old one's too small. It barely covers his tummy.
   The old one's too small. He keeps banging his head against the sides.

8. The trunk of the tree that blew over.
   A dress for the new baby.

9. As often as possible.
   As soon as possible because he needs the money.

10. I actually met Paul McCartney!
    Robert Lewandowski of Bayern Munich.

* This page is photocopiable for classroom use only.

References

Abercrombie, D. (1967). *Elements of general phonetics*. Edinburgh University Press.

Allo Allo Wiki (n.d.). *Officer Crabtree*. alloallo.fandom.com/wiki/Officer_Crabtree

Bostrom, A. (2018). *Good moaning France!: Officer Crabtree's Fronch phrose berk*. Waterside Press.

Bradford, B. (1988). *Intonation in context*. Cambridge University Press.

Brazil, D. (1997). *The communicative value of intonation in English*. Cambridge University Press.

Brazil, D., Coulthard, M. & Johns, C. (1980). *Discourse intonation and language teaching*. Longman.

Brown, A. (2000). Priorities in pronunciation teaching: Responses from Singaporean trainee teachers and international experts. In A. Brown, D. Deterding, & E. L. Low (Eds.), *The English language in Singapore: Research on pronunciation* (pp. 121–132). Singapore Association for Applied Linguistics.

Brown, A. (2014). *Pronunciation and phonetics: A practical guide for English language teachers*. Routledge.

Carney, E. (1994). *A survey of English spelling*. Routledge.

Discovery Education (n.d.). *Puzzlemaker*. http://puzzlemaker.discoveryeducation.com/WordSearchSetupForm.asp

English Spelling Society (n.d.). *Poems showing the absurdities of English spelling*. http://spellingsociety.org/uploaded_misc/poems-online-misc.pdf

Follow the Fleet (1936). RKO Radio Pictures.

Higgins, J. (2017). *Minimal pairs for English RP*. minimal- http://minimal.marlodge.net/minimal.html

Higgins, J. (2018). *English (RP) homophones*. http://minimal.marlodge.net/phone.html

Honikman, B. (1964). Articulatory settings. In D. Abercrombie, D. B. Fry, P. A. D. MacCarthy, N. C. Scott & J. L. M. Trim (Eds.), *In honour of Daniel Jones* (pp. 73–84). Longman. Also in A. Brown (Ed., 1991). *Teaching English pronunciation: A book of readings* (pp. 276–297). Routledge.

Hulme, J. (1981). *Mörder Guss Reims*. Clarkson N. Potter, Inc.

Laroy, C. (1995). *Pronunciation*. Oxford University Press.

Lexico (n.d.). *Oxford dictionaries*. www.lexico.com/definition/rhubarb

Mr. Men, Little Miss. (2020). www.mrmen.com

Pickett, W. (2004). A believable accent: The phonology of the Pink Panther. *California Linguistic Notes, 29*(1), 1–13. http://english.fullerton.edu/publications/clnArchives/pdf/picket_pink.pdf

Planchenault, G. (2015). *Voices in the media: Performing French linguistic otherness*. Bloomsbury Academic.

The Pink Panther (2006). Metro-Goldwyn-Mayer, Columbia Pictures.

The Pink Panther 2 (2009). Metro-Goldwyn-Mayer, Columbia Pictures, Robert Simonds Company.

The Pink Panther Strikes Again (1976). Amjo Productions/United Artists.

van Rooten, L. D. (1967). *Mots D'Heures: Gousses, Rames*. Viking Adult.

Wells, J. C. (2006). *English intonation: An introduction*. Cambridge University Press.

Wikipedia (n.d.). *Mr. Men*. https://en.wikipedia.org/wiki/Mr._Men

Printed in Great Britain
by Amazon